Luxury Brand Management and Heritage Revival

Luxury Brand Management and Heritage Revival

Case Studies from the Swiss Watch Industry

Pierre-Yves Donzé
and Harry Guhl

BLOOMSBURY VISUAL ARTS
LONDON · NEW YORK · OXFORD · NEW DELHI · SYDNEY

BLOOMSBURY VISUAL ARTS
Bloomsbury Publishing Plc, 50 Bedford Square, London, WC1B 3DP, UK
Bloomsbury Publishing Inc, 1385 Broadway, New York, NY 10018, USA
Bloomsbury Publishing Ireland, 29 Earlsfort Terrace, Dublin 2, D02 AY28, Ireland

BLOOMSBURY, BLOOMSBURY VISUAL ARTS and the Diana logo are trademarks of Bloomsbury Publishing Plc

First published in Great Britain 2026

Copyright © Pierre-Yves Donzé and Harry Guhl, 2026

Pierre-Yves Donzé and Harry Guhl have asserted their right under the Copyright, Designs and Patents Act, 1988, to be identified as Authors of this work.

Cover design: Estudi Puk, Barcelona
Cover image courtesy of Antiquorum

All rights reserved. No part of this publication may be: i) reproduced or transmitted in any form, electronic or mechanical, including photocopying, recording or by means of any information storage or retrieval system without prior permission in writing from the publishers; or ii) used or reproduced in any way for the training, development or operation of artificial intelligence (AI) technologies, including generative AI technologies. The rights holders expressly reserve this publication from the text and data mining exception as per Article 4(3) of the Digital Single Market Directive (EU) 2019/790.

Bloomsbury Publishing Plc does not have any control over, or responsibility for, any third-party websites referred to or in this book. All internet addresses given in this book were correct at the time of going to press. The author and publisher regret any inconvenience caused if addresses have changed or sites have ceased to exist, but can accept no responsibility for any such changes.

A catalogue record for this book is available from the British Library.

A catalog record for this book is available from the Library of Congress.

ISBN:	HB:	978-1-3505-4533-5
	PB:	978-1-3505-4532-8
	ePDF:	978-1-3505-4534-2
	eBook:	978-1-3505-4535-9

Typeset by Integra Software Services Pvt. Ltd.
Printed and bound in India

For product safety related questions contact productsafety@bloomsbury.com.

To find out more about our authors and books visit www.bloomsbury.com and sign up for our newsletters.

Contents

	List of Illustrations	vii
	Foreword	ix
	Introduction	1
1	**Bringing luxury sleeping beauties back to life**	**5**
	The objectives of reawakening brands	6
	Importance of heritage for brand management	11
	Conclusion	16
2	**The transformation of Swiss watchmaking into a luxury industry**	**17**
	Luxury startups and small firms	18
	Waves of takeovers by large conglomerates	20
	The fast growth of independent companies	25
	A statistical overview of the shift to luxury	27
	The advent of the Apple Watch and its impact	29
	New institutions to legitimize the Swiss luxury watch	30
3	**Brand management in the watch industry**	**33**
	Proto-brands in the pre-industrial era	33
	The legal protection of trademarks	34
	The birth of global brands	39
	Global luxury brands	45
	Conclusion	46
4	**The revival of vanished brands**	**49**
	Case 1: The first mover: Blancpain	52
	Case 2: The failed reawakening of Léon Hatot	60
	Case 3: German brands from Glashütte	66
	Conclusion	72

5	**Brand revival and the recovery of declining firms**	73
	Case 4: Patek Philippe	76
	Case 5: Making Chopard a jewellery brand	81
	Case 6: Revival based on a concept: Hublot	87
	Case 7: Failed attempts to relaunch sleeping beauties: Corum and Ebel	93
	Conclusion	100
6	**Creating new brands from heritage**	101
	Case 8: Breguet	102
	Case 9: British watch masters	114
	Case 10: JeanRichard	119
	Case 11: Heritage brands with a technical foundation: Czapek, Lowenthal and Pouzait	124
	Conclusion	131
	Conclusion	133
	Notes	136
	Bibliography	156
	Index	163

Illustrations

1.1 Major equity investments by Investcorp SA in luxury and fashion 9
1.2 History and heritage in brand management 15
2.1 Top largest twenty watch brands, 2006 and 2024 24
2.2 Export of Swiss watches, 1980–2023 27
2.3 Top ten largest destinations for the export of Swiss watches, as a percentage of value, 2001 and 2023 28
2.4 Patent applications related to smartwatches, by country, 2010–20 30
3.1 First eight watchmaking trademarks registered in Switzerland, 1880 35
3.2 Registration of a trademark by Favre & Andrié, 1880 36
3.3 Registration of a trademark by Favre-Leuba & Co, 1882 37
3.4 Trademark registration in the Swiss watch industry, 1890–1940 37
3.5 Advertisement for Longines Conquest, 1980 41
3.6 Advertisement Longines, 2005 47
4.1 Advertisement for Blancpain, 1957 53
4.2 Advertisement for Blancpain, 1994 57
4.3 Advertisement for Blancpain, 2010 58
4.4 Presentation of the relaunch of Léon Hatot in Europa Star, 2004 61
4.5 New Léon Hatot watch presented to the public in 2008 64
4.6 Tourbillon watch developed by Lange & Söhne, 2006 69
4.7 Glashütte Original watch launched in 2002 70
5.1 Advertisement by Patek Philippe & Cie, 1943 80
5.2 Advertisement for Chopard, 1988 83
5.3 Jewellers at the Cannes Festival, 1998 85
5.4 Advertisement for Hublot, 1980 88
5.5 Advertisement for Hublot, 2005 92

5.6	Advertisement for Corum, 1980 94	6.6	Report on Graham, 2013 118
5.7	Advertisement for Ebel 98	6.7	Grand TV Screen developed by JeanRichard, 2003 121
6.1	Advertisement for Rolex using Breguet's Marie-Antoinette watch, 1953 103	6.8	Advertisement for JeanRichard, 2008 122
6.2	Advertisement for Breguet, 1983 106	6.9	Report on the relaunch of Czapek, 2015 126
6.3	Report on Breguet, 1996 110	6.10	Chronograph Loewenthal for Hermès, undated 127
6.4	Gross sales of Montres Breguet SA, in million francs and as a percentage of Swatch Group's watch sales, 2006–22 111	6.11	Pouzait wristwatch, 2024 128
		6.12	Pouzait wristwatch, 2024 129
6.5	Report on Arnold & Son, 2005 117	6.13	Pouzait's original escapement 130

Foreword

In an era of rapid change and evolving consumer preferences, the field of luxury brand management is at a fascinating crossroads. *Brand Revival in the Luxury Watch Industry: Case Studies in Heritage Management* explores the intricacies of how prestigious brands navigate the complexities of maintaining relevance while honouring their rich heritage.

Synonymous with precision and craftsmanship, the Swiss watch industry provides a compelling backdrop for exploring the delicate balance between tradition and innovation. In these pages, we examine case studies that highlight the strategies used by renowned brands to revive their identities and capture the hearts of a new generation of consumers.

Through meticulous analysis and insightful narrative, this book aims to illuminate the critical factors that contribute to successful brand management in the luxury sector. From rejuvenating established names to forging new paths in the marketplace, we offer a comprehensive understanding of the strategies that drive brand revitalization.

Whether you are a business student, marketing professional or luxury enthusiast, this exploration invites you to discover the lessons embedded in these case studies and understand their significance in the broader context of brand management. As we embark on this journey through the timeless elegance of Swiss watchmaking, we hope to inspire a deeper appreciation for the art and science of luxury brand revitalization.

Basel and Osaka, 26 November 2024

Introduction

In recent decades, the Swiss watch industry has experienced impressive growth. The value of watch export, including movements and parts, has increased from 6.8 billion francs in 1990 to more than 26 billion francs in 2023. During this time, the average price of a Swiss watch, including quartz and mechanical watches, has risen from 224 francs to 1582 francs.[1] This growth is based on the adoption of a luxury strategy, which became dominant after 2000.[2] Swiss watches are no longer simply precision instruments that tell the exact time but products that convey a strong cultural value.[3] The brand has become the ultimate expression of the identity of these products, representing an intangible asset that underpins the competitiveness and profitability of the companies that own them.

There are many different watch brands. Although the communication strategy of companies generally consists of insisting on their continuity over time – which contributes to reinforcing their legitimacy as the embodiment of a discourse on luxury – a large number of watch brands have undergone profound changes throughout the years. Some have disappeared before being reborn, often in a different guise, while others have undergone multiple transformations. Only a handful of brands have shown continuity in terms of ownership and management. A long-term development based on the exploitation of a similar concept is relatively rare. Among the 2023 ranking of the top twenty largest Swiss watch brands published by Morgan Stanley, only five can be considered as brands managed by the same company since their beginning (Audemars Piguet, Hermès, Richard Mille, Rolex and Swatch).[4] Although some of them have experienced major changes during their recent history, like Audemars Piguet with the launch of the Royal Oak (1972) and the appointment of François-Henry Bennahmias as CEO (2012), there have been no breaks in terms of ownership for these brands. The situation is similar for Swatch, which has made an impressive comeback since the launch of its MoonSwatch (2021), after several unsuccessful attempts to relaunch the brand. However, this success is part of the continuity of the brand's management since its creation. In comparison with these aforementioned cases, for a few other brands (Breitling, Chopard, Hublot and Patek Philippe), a change of ownership presented an opportunity to deeply reposition the brand, develop a new concept and engage in a new era of fast growth. These companies faced existential difficulties and needed a profound change to ensure their survival. Finally, half of the top twenty largest brands have been drastically transformed and repositioned in the context of their takeover and integration with a conglomerate (Bulgari, Cartier, IWC, Jaeger-LeCoultre, Longines, Officine Panerai, Omega, TAG Heuer, Tissot and Vacheron Constantin). The business model of these groups is based on exploiting a portfolio of complementary brands. Managing them requires defining a clear identity and precise positioning in relation to the group's other brands and to rivals in the same segment belonging to other groups.[5]

The relaunch of watch brands following a change of ownership therefore affects three-quarters of the twenty largest brands. Many smaller companies are also based on a similar business model. Yet, little is known about why and how these brands are relaunched. There are no studies, and watch companies communicate little on the subject. In the fashion business, media and managers often use the expression *reawakening a sleeping beauty* when they discuss the relaunch of a brand. The term is, however, ambiguous. It includes both brands that had disappeared and that no company used anymore (they were literally 'sleeping') and brands that had lost their lustre and needed new management to reawaken them.[6] Moreover, as this book will demonstrate, one can add new brands based on the exploitation of a heritage – the name of a famous artisan, for example. This semantic confusion actually results from the coexistence of various strategies, which are different in their essence to using an old brand for a modern business. As we discuss in detail in Chapter 1, the heritage of the brand is not simply its past, but a narrative based on the use of some elements of its past.

The aim of this book is to provide an analysis of brand relaunching in the watch industry. The two co-authors have pooled their respective skills – Harry Guhl's experience in relaunching a large number of watch brands and Pierre-Yves Donzé's knowledge of the industry's business history – to produce an original work that discusses the various methods used to relaunch watch brands, on the basis of numerous case studies. This work is based on the use of the watchmaking press, in particular the historical archives of *Europa Star* magazine, and on official sources relating to the registration of trademarks and companies.

The book has six chapters. The first three are introductory. They review the question of brand relaunching in general, as approached by management research (Chapter 1), the transformation of Swiss watchmaking into a luxury business (Chapter 2) and the historical development of brand management in the Swiss watch industry (Chapter 3). The next three chapters focus on the analysis of the relaunch of watch brands in three distinct cases: the revival of disappeared brands (Chapter 4), the revitalization of declining brands (Chapter 5) and the creation of brands based on the exploitation of a heritage (Chapter 6). They include numerous examples discussed in detail, including cases of failure, in order to highlight the ins and outs of these relaunches.

Chapter 1

Bringing luxury sleeping beauties back to life

Brands are the most important assets in the luxury industry. While the common resources of any company – that is, capital, humans and materials – are necessary to manufacture and sell any products, one needs a brand to build a luxury good. The *Cambridge Dictionary* defines a brand as 'a type of product made by a particular company and sold under a particular name'.[1] Companies use brands to give specific identities to their goods and to distinguish them from competitors. They are associated with particular meanings and values. Brand management, or branding, is hence the action taken by firms to build their brands and to communicate it to consumers. In the luxury industry, the management of brands requires specific techniques in order to add emotional value to the brands and to ensure that they embody a hard-to-reach dream for consumers.[2]

For many luxury brands, history, the past and tradition represent an accumulated experience that provides justification for the discourse of excellence and exceptionality, although other narratives can underpin a luxury brand, such as technological innovation (e.g. Ferrari or Richard Mille).[3] As a result, companies with strong brand identities, high added value and public awareness are keen to maintain them. But these brands are also the target of investors and entrepreneurs looking to launch their own businesses in the luxury market. Rather than building a new luxury brand oneself, which requires a unique, innovative concept and great faith in the strategy to be implemented, relaunching old brands appears to be a way of establishing oneself in this market. This may involve taking over a company in difficulty with a new brand-management strategy (Gucci, bought by Investcorp and relaunched by Tom Ford), relaunching a brand that had disappeared (Courrèges, a Parisian haute couture brand recently bought by the Pinault family), or creating a new brand in tribute to a deceased designer or craftsman (Rose Bertin, named after Marie-Antoinette's dressmaker).[4]

Before focusing on the case of the watch industry, this chapter discusses the question of brand relaunching in the luxury goods industry in general terms. Based on academic literature in management and business history, it explains the major issues involved in these relaunches, and the key role played by the concept of 'heritage' in this process. We will focus in particular on the fashion industry, where we can see a wide range of examples of brand relaunches.

The objectives of reawakening brands

Management scholars and business historians have not made a clear distinction between the 'relaunch', 'revival' and 'reawakening' of brands. All these terms are usually used synonymously when discussing the idea of developing a new business model, based on a new heritage strategy, to exploit a brand that has disappeared from the market (a vanished brand) or has lost its competitiveness (a declining brand). This practice became widespread in the fashion and luxury industry after the 1980s. This results from the mutation of this sector at that time, characterized by a triple transformation: the globalization of markets (more business opportunities for brands), the emergence of conglomerates and multinational enterprises (firms that have capital to invest massively in retail and branding), and a new marketing strategy (the advent of accessible luxury – that is, luxury goods for masses).[5] The increasing power of global brands in this new luxury business and the prospects for high profits attracted numerous businessmen and firms. However, new entrants need brands, and reawakening a sleeping beauty was seen by many as a means by which they could take part in the luxury industry.

There are three main reasons why entrepreneurs decide to relaunch a brand: (1) to fast become an actor in a market, (2) to expand one's business to new segments and new regions, and (3) to make a financial profit. We take in this section some cases from the fashion and luxury industry to discuss these various patterns.

First, the relaunch of a brand can answer a desire to become a new actor in a specific market. As establishing a new brand requires time and money, some entrepreneurs take over a declining firm or found a new company to exploit an old brand they have registered, in the hope they might achieve a competitive advantage faster. There are several examples of entrepreneurs in luxury fashion who cooperated with American or British designers to successfully relaunch a brand that had experienced limited growth until then. One of the best cases is undoubtedly Christian Dior after the appointment of John Galliano as an artistic director.[6] In 1986, Bernard Arnault acquired former Boussac Group, which used to be the largest French textile company, because it owned the couture house Dior. The business model of this small company had not changed since the 1960s: it created classical dresses for a few wealthy customers and made profits through the sales of accessories and licences. The brand image was, however, very traditional, and the company was largely unable to achieve sustainable growth. After the appointment of Galliano in 1997, Dior experienced a dramatic change. It was transformed into the expression of revolutionary creations in fashion – the opposite to how Dior himself considered fashion – and became a global brand, that is, a brand with an identity that is the same throughout the world. This relaunch enabled Arnault to become a leader in the luxury fashion market.

The reawakening of vanished brands also answers this will to establish oneself as a new actor in the fashion industry. The example of Vionnet has been analysed in detail by fashion historian Johanna Zanon.[7] Madeleine Vionnet had been one of the most renowned haute couture designers in Paris during the first four decades of the twentieth century. Her company, financially supported by Théophile Bader, owner of the department store Galeries Lafayette, was one of the most important during the interwar years.[8] However, the business was liquidated in 1940, a few months after her retirement. About fifty years later, two entrepreneurs, Guy and Arnaud de Lummen, had the idea of entering more actively into the fashion business through the relaunch of the Vionnet brand. Guy had been trained as a textile engineer and had been working in the production under an upmarket ready-to-wear licence. Having worked, in particular, for Pierre Balmain, he had the experience and knowledge related to the development of a broad range of products using a specific brand. When the licence with Balmain ended in 1988, he was looking for new business opportunities. His idea was to relaunch the name of a famous Parisian designer of the interwar years. He needed to find a name that was not registered as a brand, and discovered that Louise Chéruit, another Parisian couturier of the years 1900–30, and Madeleine Vionnet were available. He started with Chéruit and relaunched the brand without focusing much on its heritage, simply producing high-level ready-to-wear products, as he had done with Balmain. It was not a huge success. He thus adopted a different strategy for the second brand. Around 1993, he founded a new joint-stock company, Madeleine Vionnet SA, headquartered in Place Vendôme, Paris.[9] He was aware that, except for a few fashion experts, nobody knew this name. It was consequently necessary to communicate intensively about who Vionnet was and what she had done. He started launching perfumes and accessories, and opened a new boutique, before taking the decision to make a comeback to haute couture creation – thanks to the capital offered by a member of the Kuwaiti family who invested in Vionnet in 2003 and a contract with a New York-based department store. Building a heritage focused on a few iconic designs, particularly from Greek Antiquity, that Vionnet herself had used, Lummen appointed in 2006 a young Greek designer, Sophia Kokosalaki, as the creative director of the brand.[10] Vionnet was, however, unable to achieve the expected profitability. It was successfully sold to an Italian textile manufacturer (2009) and then to a Kazakh billionaire (2012).[11] The company was finally liquidated in 2018.[12] Despite its failure, this case is a good example of an entrepreneur, Guy de Lummen, trying to establish his own company on the fashion market.

Second, the relaunch of a vanished brand can offer the opportunity to diversify one's activities. The most widespread pattern in fashion is the desire for wholesalers to have their own brands and to verticalize their business – from production to distribution to retail. Many Asian companies have followed this model, as embodied by Shandong Ruyi, a Chinese textile company that aimed in the 2010s to become the 'LVMH of China'.[13] It started its move from being a supplier of clothing to a company controlling its own brand through the acquisition in 2010 of some 40 per cent of the capital of the Japanese apparel company Renown, whose brand D'Urban had been popular in Japan in the 1980s through its association with French actor Alain Delon.[14] Six years later, it took over Trinity group, a clothing wholesaler from Hong Kong that, after 2000, purchased some European fashion brands, such as Cerruti 1881, Gieves & Hawkes and Kent & Curwen.[15] Shandong Ruyi resorted to debt to make all its acquisitions and consequently faced severe financial difficulties.[16] However, this example shows how the purchase and relaunch of brands can be envisaged as a way to move upwards within the global value chain of fashion and apparel. A more balanced and successful case is offered by the Korean luxury distributor Shinsegae International, which purchased and relaunched Paul Poiret, named after one of the most innovative and famous couturiers at the beginning of the twentieth century, in cooperation with fashion designers established in Paris.[17] Its business objective of owning a brand was similar to that of Shandong Ruyi.

Third, and finally, some companies essentially target financial profit by buying or registering declining or vanished brands. The idea is to appoint a new creative director, boost sales on world markets and make profit through the sale or listing of the company. Private equity firms are specialized in such a business. They have, for example, massively invested in the Italian fashion industry, where numerous small- and medium-size enterprises lacked the financial means to grow globally. Hence, currently, the investment company Mayhoola for Investments SPC (Qatar) owns Valentino, while Roberto Cavalli and Gianfranco Ferré belong to two investors from Dubai, respectively Vision Investment Co. and Paris Group.[18] These financial firms from the Middle East follow the successful case of Investcorp SA.[19] Investcorp is an investment company founded in Bahrain in 1982 to direct the capital of its clients in the Arabian Gulf to various sectors in the United States and Western Europe. It has offices in Bahrain, New York and London. During the first twenty years of business, Investcorp had shown an average return on investment of 26 per cent per year.[20] Fashion and luxury was an important part of this business between the mid-1980s and the mid-1990s (see Figure 1.1). Investcorp took over several brands and sold them back, usually through IPO, after a few years of operations. These were the formative years of the luxury industry, and many brands with a potential high-value faced management and financial issues due to their small size. For most of them, IPO was only a step before being acquired by larger groups, such as Kering for Gucci or LVMH for Tiffany.

A simpler business model is also followed by individual investors who register the brand, make simple communication through a website and sell the brand to a company. One of the best examples is undoubtedly Arnaud de Lummen, who had been CEO of Madeleine Vionnet SA after his father relaunched the brand. Having experienced techniques to manage the reawakening of a sleeping beauty and been aware of the opportunities offered by such a business, he started his own company specializing in relaunching vanished brands after the failure of Vionnet.[21] In 2009, he registered the

COMPANY	MAIN BUSINESS	ACQUIRED	SOLD	NEW OWNER
Tiffany	Jewellery	1984	1987	IPO
Bertran-Trojan	Yacht manufacturing	1985	1988	IPO
Breguet	Watches	1987	1999	Swatch Group
Chaumet	Jewellery	1987	1999	LVMH
Gucci	Fashion	1987–1993	1995–1997	IPO
Saks Fifth Avenue	Department store	1990	1996	IPO
Ebel	Watches	1994	1999	LVMH

Figure 1.1 Major equity investments by Investcorp SA in luxury and fashion.
Source: Drafted by the authors on the basis of 'Investcorp SA', *International Directory of Company Histories*, Gale, 2004, vol. 57, pp. 179–182.

company Luvanis SA, in Luxembourg. Between 2008 and 2023, Luvanis SA protected a total of eighty-eight brands in France, most of them during the last five years.[22] These brands are primarily related to French fashion and interwar haute couture. Brands are not really relaunched, in the sense that Luvanis does not invest in engaging designers, opening stores and showing new collections. Instead, the company makes revival business plans, which are sold to investors with the brand. For example, leather goods brand Moynat, registered in 2008, was sold in 2012 to Bernard Arnault, who decided to properly relaunch it.[23] Another relevant example is the aforementioned designer brand Paul Poiret. Before the Korean luxury group Shinsegae International relaunched it, the brand was registered in France by Lummen in 2010. It took about four years to purchase the various rights related to this brand around the world before it was sold to the Korean group.[24] Hence, the business model of Luvanis is more to *reawaken* a sleeping beauty, while companies that then acquire its brands *relaunch* them. Its objective is merely financial profit.

Next, whatever the objective of reawakening brands is, one must consider the nature of the strategies used to carry out this business. Management scholars Delphine Dion and Gérald Mazzalovo have identified three main strategies adopted by luxury firms: brand revitalization, brand copying and retrobranding.[25]

First, brand revitalization is a strategy that does not use the past of the brand in the new communication. The company emphasizes the longevity and timelessness of its brand, but without any mention of its history. Hence, it does not build a clear heritage and does not strongly link the current brand with the past one. Dion and Mazzalovo give the example of Lacoste. This French company was founded in 1933 by the tennis star René Lacoste. He originally made a shirt for playing sport and diversified over the years towards accessories, but always with a focus on sportswear. The company was taken over by the Swiss group Maus Frères in 2012 and refocused in 2014 towards premium ready-to-wear without specific attention to sports. Although it uses the crocodile logo as the iconic representation of the brand, it does not use history in its brand strategy.[26]

Second, brand copying is a practice characterized by replicating the past without updating to present consumers. As time has passed between the heyday of the brand and its renaissance, the social and cultural environment has evolved. Consumers are not the same anymore. The lack of adaptation of values and of the product itself to the current society is therefore a risk. Dion and Mazzalovo examined the notable case of the French couturier Courrèges. His fashion house, opened in 1961, was characterized by the creation of modernist and futurist clothing. The brand had been supported since 1968 by capital from L'Oréal (which made perfume for it), then controlled by the Japanese textile group Itokin between 1983 and 1990. The inability to make it profitable led Itokin to sell it again to French investors, but the brand remained dormant.[27] In 2011, two new investors purchased the brand and relaunched Courrèges, using nostalgia from the 1960s and copying the styles of this decade.[28] This strategy was, however, unsuccessful. In 2018, Courrèges was acquired by Artemis, the holding company that owns the luxury conglomerate Kering.[29] The new management adopted a drastic change of strategy, shifting from brand copying to retrobranding.[30]

Retrobranding is the third reawakening strategy discussed by Dion and Mazzalovo. It embodies the most successful pattern in the luxury industry and is based on the exploitation of the heritage of the brand. The brand is associated with its past, but in harmony with the present. Heritage is a link between the present and the past. The brand adapted itself to new consumers. These authors take the example of the couturier Elsa Schiaparelli. Close to Salvador Dalí and the surrealist movement, she had her own couture house in Paris between 1926 and 1954. The name disappeared in the context of the crisis of French couture.[31] In 2007, Diego Della Valle, chairman of the Italian fashion company Tod's, acquired the brand. Six years later, he appointed a creative designer, then presented his first collections in 2014. He cultivates the surrealistic heritage of the brand to develop contemporary couture, which is presented as a tribute to the historical relations between art and fashion.[32]

Importance of heritage for brand management

The concept of heritage is at the core of the strategies for reawakening vanished brands. Its proper management has a major impact on the success of a brand's comeback on the market. Cases of failure are often the illustration of contradictions within the heritage or of the inadaptation of brand management to it. Before discussing in detail how heritage is constructed and used as a resource by companies, one must discuss its true nature. What is indeed heritage?

Very often, management scholars argue that brands have a heritage *per se* – managers often use the expression 'a brand's DNA' with a similar assumption. Each brand has a heritage, and the issue would be to explore and use it – or not. One of the most quoted articles on brand heritage management gives a positivist definition of heritage: 'a dimension of a brand's identity found in its track record, longevity, core values, use of symbols and particularly in an organisational belief that its history is important'.[33] Consequently, any brand with a past would have a heritage, but a 'heritage brand' is a brand whose values are based on the use of this heritage. The authors give an example from the watch industry:

> For example, in the watch industry, both Patek Philippe and Tag Heuer are brands with heritage. We would, however, consider Patek Philippe to be a heritage brand because it has chosen to emphasise its history as a key component of its brand identity and positioning. Tag Heuer does not; thus, we see it as a brand with a heritage, but not a heritage brand. To make heritage part of a brand's value proposition is a strategic decision.[34]

Next, this team of researchers developed the concept of a 'heritage quotient' (HQ) to measure the level to which brands have developed their heritage. HQ is based on five elements: a track record (proof that a company has, in the past, followed the values emphasized in the current time), longevity (if a brand is not old enough, it does not have any heritage), core values (that show continuity and consistency over time), the use of symbols (to embody core values) and the fact of considering history as important to the brand identity.[35] Hence, considering that brand heritage can provide a competitive advantage, these scholars advise companies to uncover and activate their heritage.

Fashion historians follow a similar approach when discussing the longevity, maintenance and relaunching of brands. Historical evidence shows that brands pursue their existence over time, as the case of Parisian haute couture clearly demonstrates.[36] In this industry, brands were born from the names of couturiers. Some early companies, like the House of Worth, became family businesses, and their name was kept over generations. For example, Charles Frederick Worth founded his company in 1858, and it was pursued by his family up to 1936, when the fourth generation closed it. Considering the renown of the name, Maison Paquin, another haute couture house that had already purchased Worth's branch in London in the 1940s, took over the entire firm in 1954. However, financial difficulties led to the closure of Paquin and Worth in Paris in 1956, and the London branch of Worth in 1967.[37] Worth's name was thus maintained over more than a century. However, there was no heritage strategy by the owners. They pursued a model of traditional haute couture (making dresses for wealthy customers). Paquin purchased the name and the boutiques in Paris and London but did not really relaunch the brand. There are numerous similar examples in the luxury industry for this period, including jewellers like Cartier and Tiffany.[38] Brands were a family asset more than a real heritage. A reputation of excellence was attached to these names, but they did not implement any heritage strategy, in the contemporary sense.

The situation started to change in haute couture following the end of the Second World War. Numerous couturier companies were small and financially unstable, however brilliant their owners may have been, and closed their houses during that time. The number of haute couture houses in Paris declined from 106 in 1946 to nineteen in 1967.[39] However, a new business model emerged in this context with the foundation of Christian Dior SA in 1946.[40] The textile entrepreneur Marcel Boussac invested lots of capital in this firm, which soon became the world's largest fashion company, and appointed managers to control its finances. It was a long-term investment and, after the sudden death of Dior in 1957, the company appointed new designers to keep the name alive. Yves Saint Laurent was the first one, but he left in 1960 because his creations were too modern and did not correspond with the image, reputation and clientele of Dior. He was replaced by a more traditional designer who fitted better with the brand's image, Marc Bohan. There was not a clear heritage yet, but there was a general understanding that there was a need to pursue a certain style to maintain the name of a creator.

Heritage appeared as a core concept in luxury fashion during the 1980s and 1990s. As explained by management scholars, a need to better connect the past and the present to offer legitimacy to brands led companies not only to better investigate their own past but also to construct a heritage – that is, a coherent narrative that places contemporary actions and creations in a historical continuity. What became important was not the veracity of the story but its *consistency*. This is exactly what Karl Lagerfeld did when he was appointed creative director of Chanel in 1983. He did not follow Chanel's history and tradition *stricto sensu* but took inspiration from some iconic designs and personal episodes of Coco Chanel's life to develop a narrative on the brand and create clothing and accessories that would embody it.[41] Bernard Arnault was probably inspired by this example when he appointed the Italian designer Gianfranco Ferré at the head of Dior in 1989. The result, however, was not satisfactory, and he was replaced by the British designer John Galliano in 1997. The latter implemented a very successful heritage strategy that transformed Dior into one of the world's most glamorous and profitable fashion brands.[42]

The example of Parisian haute couture, briefly summarized here, demonstrates that the continuity of a brand name has not always been the consequence of the existence of heritage. Heritage emerges in specific conditions, when companies need it. Some fashion historians use the concept of 'cultural capital', developed by French sociologist Pierre Bourdieu, to maintain that brands own an intangible value, even if not used by the managers of the firm. Johanna Zanon argued that 'sleeping beauty brand is the repository of objectified cultural capital'.[43] The objective of creative directors and brand managers is thus to rediscover this capital and use it to develop products and narratives that are consistent with the history of the brand. In some more extreme cases, as claimed by Delphine Dion, companies do not even exist anymore; heritage is the only (intangible) asset owned by brands, as fixed assets, such as factories, stocks and land, have disappeared.[44] Consequently, there is a largely shared belief according to which history exists and knowing it properly will help in finding the real heritage of the brand and managing it properly.

Most brand managers and CEOs share this belief and maintain that one must know a brand's 'DNA' to properly understand it. The problem with such an expression is that it rests on the belief that a brand's heritage really does exist, in the same way as the DNA of a living being. In a way, the brand is a prisoner of its heritage and must conform to it. And yet, as we all know, DNA only concerns living beings – which brands do not. Brands do not have DNA, and heritage as such does not exist. Instead, it is the result of a social construction. In luxury fashion, another narrative technique used to connect obviously disconnected styles and elements is to claim that current designers follow and make a tribute to the 'spirit' of the founder. This notion is vague enough to assert the existence of a continuity between the past and the present. This 'spirit' can be considered as another way to talk about the DNA of the brand.[45]

The works of social scientists and historians help us to understand how managers construct a heritage, consciously or not, in some specific conditions. The epistemology of history teaches us that history, as the true embodiment of the past, does not exist. The way we see and consider history in the present time is a social construction that depends on the observer.[46] History is a discourse on the past produced in the present, under specific conditions.[47] 'Real' history does not exist, because the past cannot be observed. Traces that have come down to us, including archives, objects and memories, enable us to apprehend the past. However, the narrative constructed on these traces is itself influenced by the selection of these traces and the interpretation we make of them. For example, the bombing of Hiroshima can be seen as a major event that ended the war and spared the lives of thousands of American soldiers, or as a useless show of force that destroyed the lives of tens of thousands of civilians.[48]

This discussion about the philosophy of history is important because it helps to illustrate that a brand's heritage does not exist per se. A heritage is an invented tradition, to use the words of two British historians.[49] It does not mean that there is no relation between the present and the past of a brand, and that all the narrative is a pure fiction. A heritage needs to be considered as a *bricolage* – that is, the assembly of a number of elements from the past with non-historical elements into a coherent narrative (see Figure 1.2). History is an important source of inspiration, but selecting events, personages and iconic products is as necessary as neglecting some aspects of the past in making a coherent heritage. For example, Chanel's official website presents the biography of its founder Gabrielle 'Coco' Chanel and the brand's official history but fails to mention Coco's relationship with a Nazi officer during the war and her refuge in Switzerland in 1944, as this is damaging to the image of the free, visionary woman on which the brand has built its heritage.[50] Delphine Dion has also emphasized that, even if managers have little information of the past of their brand, they can make a heritage by creating a string narrative based on the extrapolation of some historical element, as was done for the French trunkmaker Moynat after its takeover by Bernard Arnault in 2010.[51] Similarly, legendary or semi-legendary personages can be developed into historical figures to give more credibility to a heritage, as in the case of the monk Dom Perignon, presented as one of the pioneers, if not the inventor, of champagne.[52]

The second important point is that the whole heritage does not necessarily rely on the past. Some non-historical

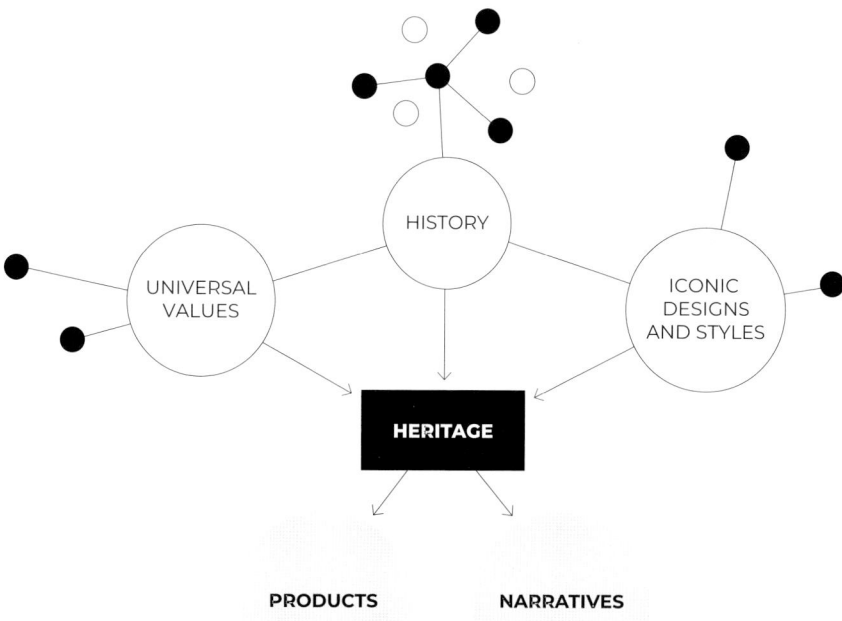

Figure 1.2 History and heritage in brand management.
Source: Drafted by the authors. © Pierre-Yves Donzé and Harry Guhl.

elements can be used and mixed with history to give more glamour or originality to the heritage. These non-historical elements can be universal values, like love and freedom, or iconic designs and styles, like the Tiffany blue, Louis Vuitton monogram or Bulgari snake. These non-historical elements are combined with the elements selected from the past into a narrative that usually does not follow a chronology. What is important is the oneiric universe proposed by the brand on the basis of its historical universe. Cartier is an excellent illustration of the construction of a heritage that transcends chronological boundaries, reinforcing the brand's timeless image. Its series of short movies, *L'Odyssée de Cartier*, blends historical figures, such as artistic director Jeanne Toussaint, the extravagance of its clientele, oriental cultural influences on its creations, the emblematic figure of the panther, love as a universal sentiment and the iconic designs of certain creations, watches and jewellery, into a poetic narrative that takes the viewer into a dreamlike universe.[53] What matters is not history and chronology but the way in which elements of the past contribute to the construction of a coherent heritage.

Conclusion

The brief review of the literature in management studies and fashion history on the subject of the revival of sleeping beauties and vanished brands provided an opportunity to discuss the concept of heritage in detail. We have shown that heritage does not exist as such. It is a social construct resulting from the actions of managers with a clear vision for their brand. This does not mean, however, that heritage is a purely invented narrative. It is inspired by elements of the past, which are blended with iconic products and universal values to offer a coherent discourse about the brand. The Swiss watch industry has drawn heavily on this heritage strategy since the 1980s, as we discuss in the next chapter.

Chapter 2

The transformation of Swiss watchmaking into a luxury industry

The Swiss watch industry has transformed itself since 2000 into a luxury industry. Of course, the luxury watch is not a new phenomenon. Watchmaking started in the seventeenth and eighteenth centuries as a business targeting wealthy people, and there have always been companies specializing in this business, as this chapter will discuss. However, until the end of the twentieth century, luxury watches constituted a niche market. The driving force behind the development of the Swiss watch industry was the mass production and distribution of watches. Then, around 2000, a new trend emerged that repositioned the Swiss watch industry into the field of luxury. Luxury Swiss watches, which used to be the exception, became the norm, enabling Swiss watch companies to surge back onto the world market as leaders and worthy competitors of Japanese firms. The change relied on two major sets of factors.

First, there were factors external to the Swiss watch industry. The European luxury industry experienced a transformation during the 1990s, and watchmaking was a part of this transformation.[1] The globalization of markets following the end of the Cold War and the advent of a new type of multinational enterprise, such as LVMH (founded in 1987), Richemont (1988) and Kering (founded in 1962 but which engaged in luxury with the takeover of Gucci in 1999) was the basis for the fast growth in the luxury business. The new business model implemented by these companies focused on accessible luxury brands – namely, brands that expressed the idea of uniqueness and social distance and were embedded in industrialized goods. Until the 1960s, the luxury industry was based on artisans and small enterprises, which manufactured, mostly by hand, small batches of high-quality goods for wealthy people. This business was characterized as exclusive luxury because only a handful of people could afford it. Cartier, Christian Dior, Louis Vuitton and Vacheron & Constantin used to work like that. However, this business model underwent a deep crisis in the 1960s due to social change and the different expectations of a new generation of wealthy classes who did not want traditional goods that expressed their wealth but attractive brands that expressed coolness and sex appeal. Most small and exclusive luxury companies could not cope with this change, but new companies like LVMH fundamentally revised their brand management and took the lead. Since the 1990s, the core of the luxury industry has based itself on accessible brands that offer an attractive message to middle classes around the globe. The Swiss watch industry has been part of this general transformation of the luxury business.

Second, there were internal factors. Watchmaking presented a particular trajectory in a transformed luxury industry. It was not a classic sector strengthened by the changes of the 1980s and 1990s but a sector of the precision instruments industry that repositioned itself in the luxury segment to regain its position as a world market leader.[2] This change was made possible by a transformation in the status of the watch. It went from a utilitarian object (precise measurer of time) to a social marker (fashionable and distinctive accessory). In this way, the Swatch played a pioneering role. Although a cheap product, it was more than a precision instrument. It was a fashion accessory that demonstrated to watch manufacturers what could be done with a watch in terms of events and storytelling, paving the way for luxury watchmaking based on products that embody narratives.

The luxury strategy pursued by Swiss watch companies since the 1990s has given rise to numerous studies in anthropology, economics and history, highlighting the sources of the industry's current success.[3] This chapter uses a business history approach to explain the stages in the transformation of a traditional manufacturing industry into a luxury industry. In the case of Swiss watchmaking, its repositioning towards luxury comprised three main stages: (1) the emergence and growth of small firms and startups; (2) the investments by large corporations; and (3) the implementation of new strategies by independent firms.

Luxury startups and small firms

The manufacturing of luxury watches was a niche market controlled by a handful of companies based in Geneva until the 1980s. Patek, Philippe & Cie is the most well-known example of such companies.[4] The roots of this company go back to a partnership signed in Geneva in 1839 by two Polish refugees, Antoni Norbert Patek and Franciszek Czapek, to make and sell watches. After

Swiss Watchmaking as a Luxury Industry

they separated in 1845, Patek formed an alliance with French watch artisan Jean Adrien Philippe. The company was small until the Second World War. From 1839 to 1900, its average output was a little less than 1,800 watches a year. It grew at the beginning of the twentieth century, reaching 6,050 watches in 1907 and producing top-of-the-range goods characterized by complicated watches and jewellery. In 1932, struggling with financial difficulties during the world recession, Patek Philippe was bought by the Stern family, which still owns it. The company was reorganized and experienced high growth during the second part of the twentieth century, with output increasing from 12,000 watches in 1970 to 20,000 in 2000.[5] The success of Patek Philippe relied on a classic and basic model of a wristwatch, the Calatrava. The Calatrava continues to be commercialized in different varieties today and, of course, standardized for machine production to ensure high profits. Adopting the same perspective, Patek Philippe also launched the casual luxury watch Nautilus (1976), which became an iconic model. At the same time, Patek Philippe developed a small series of complicated wristwatches to maintain its reputation as a traditional watchmaker. The union of excellence in manufacturing – maintained by the creation of highly complicated watches, on which the company bases its brand strategy – and the standardized production of a basic model lies at the heart of Patek Philippe's success in the world market (see Chapter 5).

Besides luxury watch manufacturers with a long tradition, jewellery watch companies from Geneva experienced growth after the Second World War. This was notably the case for Piaget.[6] This company was originally a small family workshop, set up in 1874 at La Côte-aux-Fées, in the canton of Neuchâtel, to provide watch movements to a broad range of assembly-makers. It experienced strong growth in the 1950s and 1960s thanks to the business relationships it established with famous jewellers like Garrard & Asprey in London, Tiffany in New York and Cartier in Paris, all selling Piaget watches. It opened a boutique (1959) and then a manufacturing company (1960) in Geneva. The company specialized in the manufacture of jewellery watches. However, its growth was enhanced by the liberalization of the industry, which facilitated mergers. In 1964, Piaget bought up the company Baume & Mercier, another family firm from the Jura Mountains, established in Geneva in 1920. It constituted the core of the luxury watches group, which was taken over by Richemont in 1988. Piaget focused on the luxury market, while Baume & Mercier focused on accessible products.

The example of Piaget demonstrates that a watch company with a clear position in the market and specific products can keep competitive in the world market despite the advent of Japanese watch companies and the quartz revolution. The relaunch of Chopard after its takeover by the Scheufele family (1963) (see Chapter 5), the foundation of Robergé Watches by Arab merchants based in Geneva (1972), the set-up of Raymond Weil (1976) and the production under the licence of Christian Dior watches by the small company Sofior SA (1977) are all examples of businesses developed in Geneva on the exploitation of a marketing project. This trend continued over the following decades, making Geneva a cluster of luxury startups and small companies operating beside Rolex, the world's largest watch brand. The share of Geneva among the total value of Swiss watch exports grew from 12.7 per cent in 1972 to 37 per cent in 1985.[7]

Their marketing strategy was the core competitive advantage of these luxury startups. They used their know-how of mechanical watches to sell high-value-added products that expressed the tradition of Swiss watchmaking. Watches were no longer only precision instruments but luxury accessories. One of the most successful brands during the 1980s was Blancpain, a company taken over by the Société Suisse de Microélectronique et d'Horlogerie (SMH, Swatch Group since 1998) in 1992 (see Chapter 4).

Waves of takeovers by large conglomerates

The objective of SMH was not only to have one more brand in the exclusive luxury segment but also to internalize new expertise in marketing and the production of complicated timepieces. Biver was appointed head of marketing and communications of Omega in 1993. He led the repositioning of this brand until his departure from the Swatch Group in 2003. His task was to regain the position of the world's leading top-of-the-range watch brand, held by Rolex since the 1970s.[8] Omega's repositioning represented a major step in transforming Swiss watchmaking into a luxury industry. The luxury strategy went beyond startups and small- and medium-sized companies. The transformation of Omega would show the entire industry that a new way of selling watches was possible.

Biver implemented a new marketing strategy aimed at strengthening the Omega brand as an accessible luxury product. Communication lay at the heart of this strategy. Omega moved from image advertising to message advertising, using new slogans such as *Omega, my choice* (1997). The brand became a vehicle for emotions through storytelling, with media events the crux of the policy. Thus, after a seven-year absence, Omega returned to the Basel Fair in 1993, an event it used as a platform for its new communication, organizing a space forum in the company of several renowned astronauts. Omega used its participation in the American space programme as an important communication tool. The following year, Omega again created a buzz in Basel by inviting Neil Armstrong to launch a new collection of the *Speedmaster* model – the watch that had accompanied the American astronauts to the Moon in 1969 – to mark the 25th anniversary of the first moon landing. Similar media actions were undertaken when other collections were renewed, such as the use of ambassadors like American model Cindy Crawford or tennis player Martina Hingis for the launch of a modernized *Constellation* collection in 1995.

Omega's brand renewal was driven by threefold positioning. First, Omega reinforced its image of technical excellence. For example, while Omega had given up application chronometry certificates in the 1970s (leaving this activity to Rolex), Biver decided in 1994 to return to making chronometers. Since then, Omega has shown a general upward trend, enabling it to regain market share (12.7 per cent in 1994, 14.2 per cent in 2000, and 26.9 per cent in 2010). This strategy was reinforced by the relaunch of a tourbillon model (1994) and, above all, by using a new type of escapement, the so-called co-axial escapement (1997), followed by the launch of a new Omega movement with this component (2007). For consumers, the important thing was not so much understanding the subtle workings of this new escapement but remembering that Omega was a brand that remained technically innovative. Finally, in 2008, the Swatch Group reused the Omega brand for the timekeeping of the Beijing Olympic Games. After being temporarily carried out by its competitor Seiko (Barcelona 1992), the official timekeeping of the Olympic Games was taken over by the Swatch Group's subsidiary Swiss Timing using the Swatch brand (Atlanta 1996; Sydney 2000; Athens 2004). The choice of Omega for these Games not only promoted the brand's image of technical excellence but also strengthened its presence in the Chinese market.

Second, Omega strengthened its historical legitimacy through a communication policy highlighting the brand's long history of innovation and technical excellence. The festivities to mark the 150th anniversary of the company's foundation in 1998 provided an opportunity to celebrate its historical roots, with the publication of a book of almost 500 pages that highlighted the development of sports timekeeping, the prizes won in chronometry competitions, and participation in the voyage to the Moon, among other events, as a way of combining tradition and excellence.[9]

Third, Omega's new positioning was based on glamour. While communication had focused mainly on the products themselves, Biver decided to contract celebrities to imbue his watches with more emotion. Hence, in 1995, supermodel Cindy Crawford and the fictional character James Bond became the brand's first ambassadors, soon followed by top-tier actor George Clooney. Since then, Omega has hired several actors and sports people as brand ambassadors.

The new strategy adopted by Omega in the 1990s led to a sharp increase in sales. Sales rose from around 575 million francs in 1991 to 1.3 billion by 2006 (9.7 per cent).[10] This impressive success left no one indifferent in the watch industry. Biver had demonstrated the potential offered by a luxury strategy. Not only the Swatch Group but also many newcomers (particularly from the French luxury industry) committed to this new direction. The acquisition of brands was their favourite tool for investing in the watch business.

Between 1997 and 2000, the Swatch Group developed its portfolio of brands in two main directions. First, it signed a licence contract with the US designer Calvin Klein to launch a collection of watches and entered the fashion watches segment (1997). Second, it purchased four brands in the luxury segment and positioned each in a specific segment. Breguet (taken over in 1999; see Chapter 6) was used for mechanical watches that expressed traditional manufacturing know-how; Léon Hatot (1999; see Chapter 4) was used to launch jewellery watches for women; Jaquet Droz (2000) was used for products merging mechanical tradition and modern design; and Glashütte Uhrentriebe (2000; see Chapter 4) was used as the embodiment of the German watchmaking tradition. The Swatch Group attempted to find success in the jewellery watch market through a joint venture with Tiffany (2007), but the cooperation was not satisfactory and came to an end in 2011. Finally, in 2013, the Swatch Group took over Harry Winston.[11]

At the same time, Compagnie Financière Richemont expanded its portfolio of brands beyond Cartier and Piaget. Richemont decided to refocus on luxury, with a strong focus on jewellery and watches.[12] In 1999, it acquired the French jeweller Van Cleef & Arpels and developed its collection of watches. The following year, it purchased Swiss watch companies Jaeger-LeCoultre and IWC and German company A. Lange & Söhne (see Chapter 4). All were positioned as traditional manufacturers of mechanical watches. A few years later, Richemont entered the field of fashion watches with the foundation of a joint venture with Ralph Lauren (2008). It also purchased a small company specializing in high-end modern mechanical watches, Roger Dubuis (2008). Consequently, unlike the Swatch Group, which is present in all market segments from Swatch to Breguet, Richemont has stayed focused on the luxury market. The marketing knowledge necessary to manage luxury brands came largely from France through Cartier, which has remained Richemont's core company. Most of the CEOs and managers of the brands belonging to Richemont have graduated from French schools and started their careers in Cartier. For example, Vacheron Constantin, one of the oldest Swiss watch brands, which today emphasizes its historical heritage, was headed between 2017 and 2024 by a French national, Louis Ferla, who entered Richemont in 2001 and worked for more than ten years for Cartier.[13]

Finally, one must stress the emergence of newcomers in the Swiss watch industry. French luxury companies have invested in numerous companies since the late 1990s. This applies, of course, to LVMH, the world's largest luxury conglomerate, founded in 1987.[14] In 1999, it entered the watch industry by acquiring TAG Heuer and Zenith, followed by Hublot (2008; see Chapter 5) and Bulgari (2011). The objective was to use TAG Heuer to compete against Rolex, Omega and Cartier in the lucrative accessible-luxury segment. However, this brand has been unable to find a competitive strategy. In the meantime, LVMH has used its organizational capabilities in watchmaking to develop watches for its star brand, Louis Vuitton. The first LV watch was launched in 2002. Since then, LVMH has invested massively in the development of Vuitton watches.

In the 1990s, luxury fashion watches emerged as a new trend and started to grow fast after 2000, attracting independent haute couture houses from France. Hermès is a case in point.[15] It opened a subsidiary in Switzerland to make watches in 1978, but the business did not begin to develop till the second part of the 1990s. However, by the mid-2000s, Hermès watches were mass-consumption goods using quartz movements. In 2006, the management of this company decided to move to mechanical watches and luxury. It took 25 per cent of the capital of Vaucher Manufacture Fleurier SA, a small company specializing in manufacturing mechanical movements, increasing its investment in production capacity after 2010. Chanel followed a similar development path. Although it had a collection of watches since 1987, a major step was made in 1998 with investment in the construction of a new factory and a stake in Bell & Ross, a French watchmaking company founded in 1992.[16] The move upmarket in Chanel watches was largely based on a new model of self-winding watches (J12), launched in 2000, and with some movements supplied by Audemars Piguet.

What was the result of all these investments? A comparison of the top twenty brands is a good way to stress the evolution of competitiveness in the major companies and the changing hierarchy between them (see Figure 2.1). There are five main points to emphasize. First, the combined gross sales of these twenty top brands increased dramatically from 12.8 billion francs to nearly 31.6 billion, reflecting the Swiss watch industry's refocus on luxury. Second, Rolex kept the number of positions it had held since the 1970s.[17] It maintained its marketing strategy based on the production and sale of watches that

	2006				2024		
	BRAND	**OWNER**	**SALES (MILLION CHF)**		**BRAND**	**OWNER**	**SALES (MILLION CHF)**
1	Rolex	Rolex	2.840	1	Rolex	Rolex	10.100
2	Cartier	Richemont	1.771	2	Cartier	Richemont	3.100
3	Omega	Swatch Group	1.350	3	Omega	Swatch Group	2.600
4	TAG Heuer	LVMH	822	4	Audemars Piguet	Independent	2.350
5	Patek Philippe	Independent	611	5	Patek Philippe	Independent	2.050
6	Swatch	Swatch Group	610	6	Richard Mille	Independent	1.540
7	Bulgari	Independent	457	7	Longines	Swatch Group	1.110
8	Chopard	Independent	409	8	Vacheron Constantin	Richemont	1.097
9	Audemars Piguet	Independent	372	9	Breitling	Independent	870
10	Tissot	Swatch Group	360	10	Tissot	Swatch Group	825
11	Gucci	Independent	356	11	IWC	Richemont	726
12	IWC	Richemont	356	12	Hublot	LVMH	670
13	Breguet	Swatch Group	350	13	Swatch	Swatch Group	660
14	Jaeger-LeCoultre	Richemont	348	14	Jaeger-LeCoultre	Richemont	641
15	Frank Muller	Independent	340	15	TAG Heuer	LVMH	615
16	Longines	Swatch Group	325	16	Hermès	Independent	593
17	Rado	Swatch Group	305	17	Tudor	Rolex	645
18	Piaget	Richemont	284	18	Officine Panerai	Richemont	520
19	Vacheron Constantin	Richemont	277	19	Bulgari	LVMH	445
20	Raymond Weil	Independent	253	20	Chopard	Independent	420

Figure 2.1 Top largest twenty watch brands, 2006 and 2024.

Source: Drafted by the authors on the basis of Vontobel (2006) and Morgan Stanley (2024).

embody individual success and excellence. This company was even able to strengthen its competitiveness. By 2024, it had become three times as large as the no. 2, Cartier, when in 2006 it had not even been twice as big. Moreover, Rolex actively developed its second brand, Tudor, in a lower segment to prevent competitors, particularly Longines and TAG Heuer, from getting too strong and ambitious and moving upward to challenge Rolex.

Third, the Swatch Group showed a relative decline. While it had six brands in the top twenty in 2006, it dropped to four by 2024. Rado and Breguet disappeared, while the position of Swatch declined. This group has faced difficulties in developing exclusive luxury brands. Today, its competitiveness relies on accessible luxury and mass-market brands. Fourth, although French luxury fashion brands made an impressive entry into the Swiss watch industry, they are still small players. Neither Chanel nor Louis Vuitton are ranked, and Hermès is the only one still present in 2024. LVMH is better represented by Bulgari and traditional Swiss watch brands. Fifth, independent brands present a dramatic expansion. They are the real winners of repositioning the Swiss watch industry on luxury. Besides Rolex, one can mention Audemars Piguet, Richard Mille and Patek Philippe, which all have sales above 1 billion francs in 2024. The next section discusses the source of their competitiveness.

The fast growth of independent companies

There is no single issue that explains the strong growth of independent watchmakers over the last twenty years, but the most successful brands are all characterized by products with a strong identity, on which this growth is largely based. These products have built up competitive marketing strategies and maintained them over the long term.

This is clearly the case with Rolex, whose competitive advantage is based on a series of models developed between 1931 (Oyster Perpetual) and 1963 (Daytona Chronograph) that embody technical excellence and the exceptional nature of those who wear them. Apart from the Sky-Dweller world calendar watch, launched in 2012 but with the brand's aesthetic codes, there has been virtually no product innovation to date. Moreover, Rolex has essentially not changed its strategic positioning (the watch as an expression of social status). On the other hand, it has invested heavily in buying out its suppliers and expanding internationally, particularly in China. According to Euromonitor International, Rolex was still only the third-largest watch brand in the Chinese market in 2016 but was set to become the largest by 2021.[18] Strong global demand for Rolex watches has led to a dramatic increase in production, from around 635,000 pieces in 2000 to over 1.2 million in 2023.[19]

In the field of mechanical watches, which embody the Swiss manufacturing tradition, Patek Philippe has also pursued a strategy that has been successful since the 1950s and 1960s – namely, a limited series of wristwatches with grand complications that express the brand's watchmaking genius, and the maintenance of a few collections of simple watches of refined design, sold as sports watches with large margins, such as the Calatrava (1934) and Nautilus (1976) models. The Nautilus in particular has become such an icon that Patek Philippe, after deciding to discontinue production in 2021, launched a similar model in 2024, the Cubitus. Finally, it should be noted that, despite the fact that Patek Philippe regularly insists on remaining an artisanal company, the volume of its watches increased 3.5-fold between 2000 (around 20,000 pieces) and 2023 (around 70,000 pieces).[20]

Finally, let's take a brief look at the dramatic development of Audemars Piguet (AP). This family firm, founded in 1875 as a manufacturer of complicated movements and watches, remained relatively small until the beginning of the twenty-first century. In 2000, it produced about 15,000 watches a year, earning an estimated 140 million francs in gross sales. Half of the sales came from the Royal Oak model, one of the first luxury watches made from steel and dubbed a 'luxury sports watch'. AP relied on the manufacturer Jaeger-LeCoultre, in which it had a 40 per cent stake in the late 1980s, for the supply of specific components.[21] Although the company invested in the verticalization of its production, selling its stake in Jaeger-LeCoultre to Richemont in 2000, and launched new versions of the Royal Oak, its growth was still limited when François-Henry Bennahmias was appointed CEO in 2012. A former professional golfer turned market developer for AP, he adopted a strategy of exclusive luxury, focusing on the Royal Oak model (nearly 90 per cent of gross sales in 2023). He drastically reduced the number of boutiques (373 in 2015 and 97 in 2023) to enhance exclusivity and increased massively the average price of AP watches (20,700 francs in 2012 and 45,000 francs in 2023). Moreover, AP became one of the first Swiss watch brands to adopt a successful 'minority management' strategy. The cooperation with Jay-Z and Black American celebrities contributed to making AP a highly desirable brand for new generations of affluent young people who are sensitive to the narrative of minority inclusion. Consequently, the sales of the company reached 2.3 billion francs and 51,000 watches in 2023.[22] This impressive development relies on the proper exploitation of an iconic model, the Royal Oak. Other brands, particularly Richard Mille and Hublot, followed a similar path.

Swiss Watchmaking as a Luxury Industry

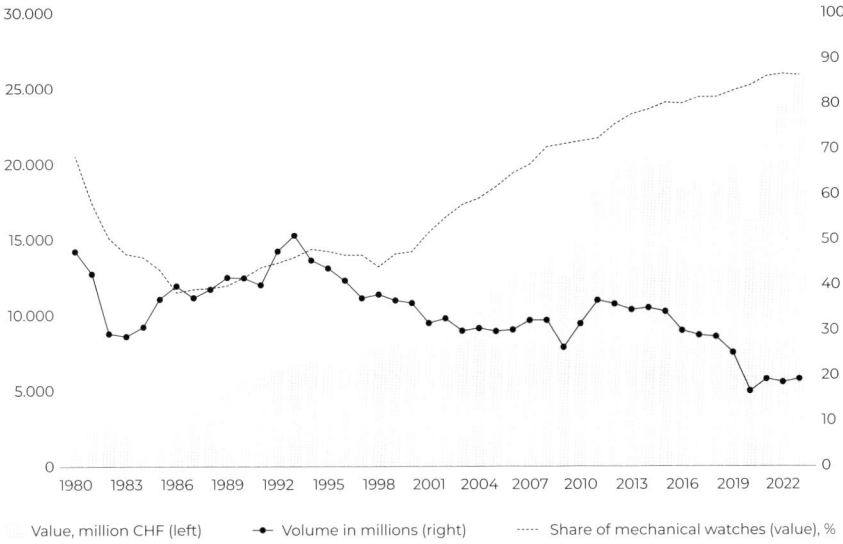

Figure 2.2 Export of Swiss watches, 1980–2023.
Source: Drafted by the authors on the basis of statistics provided by the Federation of the Swiss Watch Industry.
Note: The data includes movements.

A statistical overview of the shift to luxury

The Swiss trade statistics complement the information given in the sections above about the various companies, offering a macroeconomic perspective on the significance of such a change (see Figure 2.2). First, the long-term evolution of the export of watches highlights very well the impact of the first part of the crisis, characterized by a stagnation in value and a decline in both the volume and share of mechanical watches. Then, the period 1986–2000 shows the beginning of a comeback. The value multiplied nearly threefold because of the success of the Swatch until the mid-1990s (which led to a growth in volume, peaking at almost 51 million watches in 1993) and the comeback of mechanical watches (39 per cent of the value in 1986 and 47 per cent in 2000), which symbolize tradition and heritage – namely, a luxury strategy.

However, the shift to luxury accelerated after 2000. Despite some fluctuations, the volume of watches continued its long-term decline after the peak of popularity of the Swatch. In 2023, Switzerland exported only 19.5 million watches, the lowest level since the end of the Second World War. But, at the same time, the value experienced a huge growth, overcoming the 15 billion franc mark in 2008, 20 billion in 2012, and 25 billion in 2023. Fewer watches for more monetary value expressed the refocus on luxury. The share of mechanical watches (namely, products that embody luxury) had increased to 86 per cent of the value by 2023.

Finally, the evolution of the main markets between 2001 and 2023 made it possible to highlight which countries were the basis for the refocus on luxury (see Figure 2.3).

While the United States kept its position as the largest market for Swiss watches, one must stress the emergence of new countries, particularly China. In 2001, this market was basically non-existent for Swiss watchmakers (5.1 million francs); it is now the second largest. Moreover, one must consider that Chinese consumers are global shoppers. They represent a significant, if impossible to estimate, share of people behind Hong Kong and major European countries. As a result, the Swiss watch industry, repositioned as a luxury industry, now depends largely on China. This could become a high risk in the case of a sudden political change or a recession in this country. The Swatch Group is a case in point. This company entered China early, thanks to cooperation with a local company that dominated the retail of watches in the Chinese market and to a massive promotion of the brand Omega during the Beijing Olympics. Between 2008 and 2014, its gross sales grew from 5.7 billion francs to a peak of 8.7 billion, and the share of the Greater China region (including Hong Kong and Taiwan) went from 23 per cent to 37 per cent. By 2023, gross sales amounted to 7.9 billion, and the share of China had declined to 33 per cent.[23] Hence, the strong dependency on China had a negative impact on the Swatch Group – for example, when the government implemented an anticorruption policy or when the Chinese economy entered a phase of decline after the Covid-19 pandemic.

2001		2023	
COUNTRY	SHARE (%)	COUNTRY	SHARE (%)
United States	14.9	United States	16.6
Hong Kong	14.2	China	11.0
Japan	9.9	Hong Kong	9.4
Italy	7.9	Japan	7.3
Germany	7.3	United Kingdom	7.0
France	6.7	Singapore	6.6
United Kingdom	4.8	Germany	5.4
Singapore	4.1	France	5.1
Spain	3.2	UAE	5.0
Taiwan	1.8	Italy	4.3

Figure 2.3 Top ten largest destinations for the export of Swiss watches, as a percentage of value, 2001 and 2023.

Source: Drafted by the authors on the basis of data provided by the Federation of the Swiss Watch Industry.

The advent of the Apple Watch and its impact

Before concluding this analysis of the transformation of the Swiss watch industry since 2000, it is necessary to discuss the case of smartwatches (connected watches) and their impact. This new type of wrist-worn device is distinguished by the fact that it offers a multitude of services and functions linked to the smartphone, in addition to simply measuring time. These new products first appeared in the late 2000s, but it was not till the launch of the Apple Watch in 2015 that they became increasingly popular. Still discreet in 2010, connected watches reached an estimated market of around 45 million pieces in 2018 and more than 60 million in 2019. According to the consulting firm Counterpoint, connected watches reached a market estimated at around 100 million units by 2020 and 127 million units by 2023.[24] The market is still dominated by the Apple Watch, although its share has declined over time with the launch of smartwatches by Samsung and Chinese companies. It was estimated to be 65 per cent of all connected watches in 2015 and approximately 30 per cent in 2023.[25]

In terms of volume, connected watches still have a relatively small impact on the global watch industry, with an estimated 1.4 billion pieces produced annually. However, the Apple Watch, in particular, directly influences a specific market segment in which several of the world's largest watch companies are positioned: the mid-range segment. The decline in exports of such Swiss watches corresponds exactly to its launch in 2015. Clearly, this new product is having a negative impact on a specific category of Swiss watches. On the other hand, it is not possible to observe any direct influence on the decline of entry-market watches, where the decline is part of a long-term trend. As shown in Figure 2.1, the decline in the volume of Swiss watch exports started in the mid-1990s. The impact of the Apple Watch on Swiss watchmaking should, therefore, not be overestimated, although it is real.

The world's leading watch companies are not standing idly by in the face of this threat. TAG Heuer, for example, in cooperation with Google and Intel, launched its own connected watch in 2017, inspiring the other brands of the LVMH group to do the same in the following years, while Citizen has internalized the skills relating to this new technology with the takeover of Frédérique Constant in 2016.[26] As for the Swatch Group, it has developed its own smartwatch internally, which it has used for the Tissot brand since 2020. While it is too early to evaluate, even roughly, the real impact of Apple Watch on the evolution of the global watch industry, it is clearly a new competing product and a new technology that the old watch companies cannot ignore.

COUNTRY	N	%
China	15,614	34.34
USA	13,136	28.89
South Korea	8,415	18.51
Japan	3,432	7.55
Taiwan	1,070	2.35
Germany	553	1.22
Switzerland	385	0.85
Canada	330	0.73
Finland	278	0.61
Netherlands	263	0.58
Others	1,988	4.37
TOTAL	45,464	100

Figure 2.4 Patent applications related to smartwatches, by country, 2010–20. Source: Donzé, Borel & Porier (2022).

A study of the patents related to smartwatches registered worldwide between 2010 and 2020 has emphasized that innovation for this product was essentially realized outside Switzerland.[27] More than 45,000 patents have been identified. They were registered essentially in China, the United States and South Korea. These three countries together have more than 80 per cent of patents (see Figure 2.4). The ranking by country shows the domination of Korean firms Samsung (3,345 patents) and LG (2,055), as well as Apple (1,767). Other major applicants are not watch companies; they are firms engaged in IT business (Google, Microsoft), communication (Huawei, Nokia) and electronic components (Qualcomm, Intel). The Swatch Group was the only Swiss company to have more than 100 patent applications (102 patents). The difference in the scope of research between the Swatch Group and the firms that dominate the smartwatch business demonstrates that Swiss watch companies are not established as the new leaders in this market, at least from a short-term perspective.

New institutions to legitimize the Swiss luxury watch

The repositioning of the Swiss watch industry towards luxury is not only the result of applying a luxury strategy at the company or group level. Collective action aimed at promoting the Swiss watch as a vehicle for cultural heritage and manufacturing tradition has had a decisive influence. New collective institutions were created in Geneva, making the city the capital of luxury watchmaking.[28] The first is the Geneva Watchmaking Grand Prix (GPHG), an event founded in 2001 by Gabriel Tortella, co-founder of the watch auction house Antiquorum, and journalist Jean-Claude Pittard, both co-founders in 1979 of *La Tribune des Arts*, a magazine celebrating the excellence of traditional Geneva watchmaking. The aim of the GPHG is to 'salute the excellence of the world's watchmaking productions and annually reward the best creations and the most outstanding players in the watchmaking world'.[29] This event, which attracts a great deal of media attention, is a major event that helps to strengthen the position of Swiss watchmaking as a luxury brand.

Secondly, we should mention the relaunch of the voluntary Bureau de contrôle des montres, known as the Poinçon de Genève. This institution, created at the end of the nineteenth century with the aim of supporting local, artisanal-quality production owed its survival after the Second World War to the Patek Philippe company. However, it entered a phase of decline in the 1980s. It experienced a revival in the 1990s, with a general upward trend in the number of certifications, from 7,000 a year in 1990 to around 30,000 a year since the late 2000s. The revival of this institution owes much to Richemont, which certifies a growing proportion of its production.[30]

Thirdly, the Fondation de la Haute Horlogerie (FHH), set up in 2005 by Richemont and two independent companies (Girard Perregaux SA, which was taken over by Kering in 2011, and Audemars Piguet SA), aims to raise the profile of Swiss luxury watchmaking through a wide range of activities, such as the Salon International de la Haute Horlogerie, held in Geneva between 1990 and 2019, the organization of exhibitions in the world's major museums, and the publication of historical works. Cartier introduced the concept of 'haute horlogerie' to Switzerland in the early 1990s. Inspired by French haute couture, it aims to establish the Richemont brands as the true representatives of luxury – mainly in the face of the Swatch Group brands – but the concept is widely debated because of the semantic vagueness it embodies.

Chapter 3

Brand management in the watch industry

This chapter discusses the historical evolution of brand management in the Swiss watch industry. The reawakening of sleeping beauties and the relaunch of brands is essentially a phenomenon that developed after 1980, in the specific context of the transformation of watch-making from a manufacturing to a luxury industry.[1] However, in order to properly understand the intangible asset that watch brands are, it is necessary to go back to the history of brand management in this industry. The nature of the brand, its identity and the way it was managed by its owners changed drastically over time. This evolution can be divided into four main phases: proto-brands, trademarks, global brands and global luxury brands.

Proto-brands in the pre-industrial era

Brands exist because they fulfil a special function on the market: they represent information, related to the nature of the product and its manufacturer, transmitted to the customer. In traditional societies, when the relation between the producer and the customers was direct and realized within local communities in which both partners knew each other, products did not need a specific brand name. The transaction was realized on the basis of trust.[2]

Distance was the determinant that led to the emergence of a need to adopt new tools to communicate to customers and to distinguish themselves from their competitors. Although most scholars argue that brands were born with the industrial revolution and the adoption of laws to protect intellectual property, some business historians have developed the concept of a 'proto-brand' to demonstrate that merchants and producers have used logos and names to sell their products since antiquity. These proto-brands were not protected by any legal institutions but were broadly used to emphasize, in particular, the origin and the quality of goods.[3] Their existence was acknowledged throughout the world, and the growth of international trade was an opportunity to develop their use.[4]

Swiss watchmakers are an illustration of the adoption of proto-brands before industrialization. The limited size of the domestic market led Swiss watch manufacturers and merchants to cross borders and visit various foreign markets, first in neighbouring European countries, then, from the eighteenth century, in the Orient and the Americas. This geographic distance was probably the most important factor that led some producers to sign their watches with the name of the company. Not all Swiss watches exported before 1880 bear the signature of their producer; simple and low-quality products were often anonymous. However, high-quality and richly decorated watches usually had the name of their maker on the dial or the case. Vacheron & Constantin and Patek Philippe & Cie are probably the best examples, although there are many others, including long-defunct names that have been revived by modern entrepreneurs since the 1980s.

Moreover, one must add that Swiss watch manufacturers did not benefit from a legal instrument to protect their trademarks and brands until 1880. Some cantons had introduced some measures to protect brands through specific laws, like Berne (1849) and Geneva (1862), but the protection was basic and limited locally. The nature of the brand was not defined by the law.[5]

The legal protection of trademarks

The legal protection of intellectual property increased considerably during the last two decades of the nineteenth century. Numerous countries adopted legislation to protect patents and brands, mostly under pressure from private companies that wanted to benefit from such an instrument. In 1883, eleven countries, including Switzerland, signed the Paris Convention on the protection of intellectual property (patents, trademarks, designs and utility models). It was one of the first international treaties that extended this kind of legal protection over national borders.[6]

The advent of large, modern enterprises played a major role in this process. Companies began to adopt brand management in the late nineteenth century when their markets expanded geographically.[7] The transformation of the distribution system, with the emergence of chain stores and supermarkets, and the enlargement of consumption led to a need to identify products, especially in the consumer goods industry (processed food, beverages, tobacco, etc.). Yet despite the fact that packaged consumer goods manufacturers, like Heinz, Kellogg's or Nestlé, spread worldwide and built up a global organization during the years 1880–1914, this did not lead to the appearance of global brands. Geoffrey Jones emphasized that 'most multinationals owned numerous local or regional brands in different markets'.[8] He also showed that for Western cosmetic companies, which extended into different cultural environments in the interwar years, such as Asia, 'the extent of local adaptation of brands ... was a major marketing challenge'.[9] Stefan Schwarzkopf developed a slightly different point of view, arguing that advertising agencies played a major role in conceptualizing branding for manufacturing firms as early as the years 1890–1930, and that they developed in particular 'the idea of the global brand'.[10]

In Switzerland, the protection of trademarks (a name or a design that identifies a product) was adopted in 1879.[11] Watchmakers played an important role in the adoption of this legal instrument. Around 1876, a total of 152 of them asked the federal government to make a law on trademarks.[12] After three years of debate, the Federal Parliament accepted, in October 1879, the project of law proposed by the government. The law was enforced in April 1880. It became possible to register a trademark at a federal office and consequently obtain legal protection for a period of fifteen years. The law was revised in 1890 and amended several times in the years that followed, but its basic principle – the ability to protect a trademark – remained unchanged.

Watchmakers made fast and broad use of this new legal instrument. The first registrations started on 1st November 1880, and they had already protected a total of 116 trademarks by the end of the year.[13] It included not only complete watches but also a large variety of parts. Figure 3.1, which shows the first eight trademarks protected by watchmakers, is a good expression of this variety. These companies did not register only their names – which can be considered

NAME	PLACE	PRODUCT
Agassiz Fils	Saint-Imier	Movements and cases
J. Bastard & Redard	Geneva	Glasses
Chavanne Frères	Bienne	Watches
A. Huguenin & Fils	Le Locle	Watches and chronometers
Auguste Vuille & Fils	La Chaux-de-Fonds	Watches
Ph. Dubois & Fils	Le Locle	Back covers and movements
J. M. Badollet & Cie	Geneva	Movements and cases
Henri Capt	Geneva	Watches and jewellery

Figure 3.1 First eight watchmaking trademarks registered in Switzerland, 1880.
Source: MIH, *Archives de l'horlogerie*, volume 1, 1892, p. 24.

Figure 3.2 Registration of a trademark by Favre & Andrié, 1880.
Source: MIH, *Archives de l'horlogerie*, volume 1, 1892.

as the brand – but also a design used to identify their products and to communicate directly to customers. Even if the targeted market was overseas, it was necessary to register the trademark in Switzerland to avoid imitation and copying by a neighbouring watchmaker. For example, in 1880, the watch merchants Favre & Andrié, in Le Locle, registered their brand Favre Brandt Locle with a design mentioning the addresses of their branches in Yokohama and Osaka in the Japanese language, Japan being their main market (see Figure 3.2). Similarly, in 1882, Favre-Leuba & Co., a company specializing in the Indian market, used an elephant as a symbol (cf. Figure 3.3).

The annual registration of trademarks by Swiss watchmakers experienced a period of fast growth during the first twenty-five years (cf. Figure 3.4). It amounted to a total of 349 in 1905. It had the reached a peak slightly above 300 new trademarks each year – except during the First World War – but started to decline in the 1930s, due to the economic crisis, and stayed low in 1940. This demonstrates that the registration of trademarks was closely related to the state of demand on world markets. New brands were launched in the context of increasing demand, with watchmakers trying to address special segments and distinguish themselves from the competition. The transfer of trademarks

Brand Management in the Watch Industry

Figure 3.3 Registration of a trademark by Favre-Leuba & Co, 1882.
Source: MIH, *Archives de l'horlogerie*, volume 1, 1892.

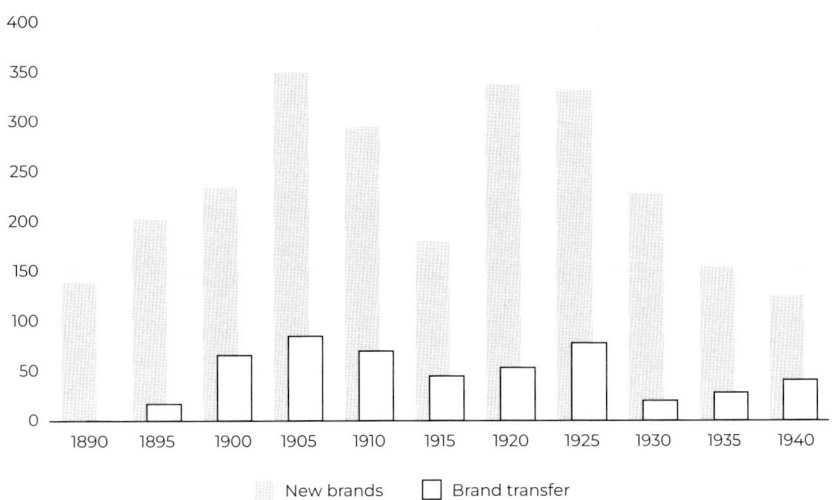

Figure 3.4 Trademark registration in the Swiss watch industry, 1890–1940.
Source: MIH, *Archives de l'horlogerie*, 1890–1940.
Note: The number of brand transfers in 1890 is unknown. This data includes Swiss and foreign brands registered in Switzerland.

also appeared after 1890. Until 1940, it fluctuated without any significant trend (between 8.5 per cent and 32.3 per cent of new registrations). However, these transfers were mostly realized in the context of the transmission of the firm, between its old and its new owners. Nothing indicates that there was a real market to sell and buy successful brands.

The largest manufacturers, which had introduced the mass production of watches, made a specific use of this new legal instrument. Like the industrial firms of the food and consumer goods industry mentioned above, these watch companies needed a strong brand, instead of the mere name of the company, to develop advertising and communication on a large scale. The trademarks Longines (1889), Omega (1894), Zenith (1897) and Rolex (1908) were registered in this context.[14] The mass production and worldwide mass distribution of watches gave way to the adoption of a new marketing strategy, especially a desire to differentiate products on the world market and to ensure that consumers could identify them easily, through advertisement and branding.[15]

These brands were new. They had to be based on contemporary concepts that embodied the technical features of the products. The idea of tradition and tribute to the creators of the past, which was to be found in the revival of the vanished and declining brands, was absent from the thinking of this formative period. Brand management was totally focused on the present and the future.

The appearance of brands in the Swiss watch industry did not lead to the standardization of products, as was the case in most other manufacturing sectors. Watch companies used the same brand to sell products whose design sometimes differed substantially from one market to another, depending on the needs and tastes of local customers.[16] For a given brand, such as Omega or Longines, watch design, price and style differed considerably from one country to another. Yet this was not a contradiction in terms of brand management. Until the advent of electronic watches in the 1970s, the competitiveness of firms in this business relied on the precision and durability of products, not their tangible design (style of the product). Whatever its appearance, a watch's brand name referred directly to its precision (i.e. movement quality). In this sense, Omega and Longines can be understood as global luxury brands because they embodied high precision, which made them top-of-the-range goods. Customers throughout the world admired – and purchased – these watches because their names were synonymous with quality. This was their competitive advantage.

A second important institutional change that impacted brand management in the watch industry during this period is the regulation of the indication of country of origin.[17] The mention of a Swiss origin on watches was, however, not the result of laws adopted in Switzerland, but in some countries willing to protect their national industries against the import of foreign goods. The first regulations regarding countries of origin were adopted in the United Kingdom (the *Merchandise Marks Act, 1887*) and the United States (the McKinley *Tariff Act, 1891*). They were protectionist, serving to inform British and American customers on the foreign origins of goods and thereby promote the consumption of domestic products.[18] These measures affected Swiss watch manufacturers. During the years following the introduction of the *Merchandise Marks Act*, the Swiss consulate in London reported that the import and sale of Swiss watches in the United Kingdom were in decline.[19] The exporters of Swiss watches without indications of origin or bearing indications with some erasable material incurred confiscations or fines.[20] However, official export statistics reflect something different. The value of finished watches exported from Switzerland to the United Kingdom amounted to 13.3 million Swiss francs in 1889. The figure went on to reach 15.2 million in 1890, 16.7 million in 1891, 15 million in 1892 and 14.1 million in 1893.[21] Consequently, the decrease of trade mentioned by the consulate and Swiss exporters before 1892 was not a fact but rather an imagined decline. Moreover, the slight decrease in the years 1892 and 1893 did not relate specifically to the origin of watches; the Swiss watch industry faced a general recession in these years before rebounding in 1895. Competition was mostly based on price – and brands for the upper level.

The birth of global brands

Global brands, namely brands that do not vary between countries and that carry the same identity around the world, appeared after the Second World War. American multinational enterprises, such as Coca-Cola or McDonald's, played a key role in this process. However, this was not a unidirectional trend, and other multinationals, particularly in daily consumer goods like Unilever and Procter & Gamble, continued to manage large portfolios of regional brands.[22] The idea of the emergence of a globalized and homogenized world market was popular in the United States in the early 1980s, as embodied by the iconic article published by Ted Levitt, professor of marketing at Harvard Business School, entitled 'The Globalization of Markets'.[23]

In most industries, however, the adaptation to regional markets was far more important than standardization.[24] Moreover, even when a company built a global brand, brand image and content could vary from one market to another – sometimes considerably – so one must discuss what the basis of global brands is, what makes them global. In the case of the cosmetic industry, Geoffrey Jones maintained that, on the one hand, there appeared 'a major homogenization of beauty ideals which the beauty companies helped diffuse'[25] that gave birth to some global brands, while on the other hand 'the persistence of distinctive local consumer preferences' is important even for companies whose organization is global, like L'Oréal or Procter & Gamble.[26] Using the example of the beverage industry, Teresa da Silva Lopes showed that the construction of real global brands is a relatively recent phenomenon, which accelerated in the 1990s, in relation to cross-border mergers and acquisitions (M&A).[27]

The Swiss watch industry is an excellent embodiment of the limited emergence of global brands after the Second World War. Although the largest manufacturers continued to sell different types of watches to different markets, in order to adapt to various local demands, they started to develop specific collections for all markets for their high-quality watches. These new products had a strong visual identity – that is, it was easy to identify them – and carried a special name – a sub-brand. Omega was one of the first movers in this new way to develop products. In 1940, it was one of the first Swiss watch manufacturers to set up a design department, entrusted to a young designer, René Bannwart, and successively launched the Seamaster collection for water-resistant watches (1948), the Constellation collection for wristwatch chronometers (1952) and the Speedmaster collection for chronographs (1957).[28] Rolex had a similar strategy, with the development of the Rolex Oyster Datejust (1945), followed by the Submariner (1953), the Explorer (1953), the GMT Master (1954), the Day-Date (1956) and the Daytona (1963).[29]

The case of Compagnie des Montres Longines is an excellent example of the way such new collections were developed.[30] In 1954, this company marketed its first self-winding watch under the sub-brand Conquest (see Figure 3.5). This new choice reflected a desire to differentiate the product on the world market. Longines' commercial directors selected 'a name with a pleasant sound, easy to pronounce in all languages'[31] and appropriate for a product positioned as a luxury good, for which the company launched for the first time a 'worldwide advertisement'[32] – that is, an advertising campaign that did not differ between countries. As the Conquest watch was an immediate hit throughout the world, other sub-brands were launched in the second half of the 1950s, like Silver Arrow (1955), 'a watch for young people, for the modern generation',[33] or Flagship (1957), for 'absolutely sensational goods'.[34] These different models marked a major innovation in terms of product development and brand strategy. From this point onwards, agents and importers were no longer all-powerful figures who conferred the design and style they wanted on Longines watches. The new marketing strategy led to a strengthening

Figure 3.5 Advertisement for Longines Conquest, 1980.

Source: *Europa Star Europe*, no. 121, 1980, p. 48 (c) Archives Europa Star.

Note: As the Conquest sub-brand was launched to embody watchmaking excellence by Longines, this company used quartz movements in the early 1980s to maintain the strong relation of this collection with precision.

of vertical integration. Headquarters began to decide directly and to control brand identity and management. This change also reflected a desire to reduce dependency on the American market and extend business to other markets around the world.

Longines conducted its first modern marketing plan during this period, which covered inter alia product development, sub-brand choice and a global advertising campaign. Since 1955, its advertising on world markets has been characterized by the standardization of logo and slogan ('the privilege of elites'). The name Longines was accompanied on ads by words like 'accuracy', 'quality' and 'style'. Then, in November 1956, the board of directors declared that due to 'the need to give a special name to a larger number of products, we have registered a set of names'.[35] At the time, however, it was not limited to the registration of the first global brands but also covered the protection of Longines' brand name against copies. During the 1950s, the brands registered by Longines included counterfeited names (Sangines 1952; Longer 1952; Lorgir 1952).[36]

Consequently, while Longines used to export only movements to its clients, who assembled them with cases made locally, it shifted gradually to the export of complete watches – special products bearing a global sub-brand. Between 1946 and 1957, the share of movements in the total volume of sales dropped from 75.6 per cent to 58 per cent.[37] However, these were large shares, and the strategy of launching global sub-brands was limited to the luxury segment. At the same time, Longines kept on exporting movements, a practice that was widespread in the Swiss watch industry at the time. In addition, the following decades were characterized by a decline in brand registrations and the development of contracts with foreign partners for licensed production. Longines registered only four brands in the 1960s and two in the 1970s. As for licensing contracts, these were primarily signed with American and South Korean firms. In the United States, the multinational company Westinghouse Electric took over the distribution company Longines-Wittnauer in 1970 and signed a contract in 1975 for 'the right to use Longines brand for American solid state watches [electronic watches], against the payment of royalties'.[38] Since then, most of the Longines watches sold on the American market have been assembled in a workshop in Puerto Rico.

The situation was very similar in South Korea, a country subject to strict limits on watch exports. Longines signed a licensing agreement with Samsung Watch Co., a joint venture co-founded in 1983 by the Korean industrial group Samsung and the Japanese watchmaker Seiko. This company assembled Longines watches with movements imported from Switzerland, as well as other watches with Seiko movements, sold under the brand name Kappa.[39] This cooperation with Swiss and Japanese watch companies enabled Samsung to establish itself as a leader on the Korean watch market in the 1990s.

The Longines experience in brand management from the 1880s through the 1980s reflects the change in the meaning of global brand identity over time. Since the late nineteenth century, Longines watches had been recognized worldwide as high-quality goods, and their competitive advantage relied on their accuracy, not their design, image or price. Hence, Longines was a global luxury brand that signified precision. However, if only this aspect is emphasized, the brand cannot be distinguished from other high-quality products made by its direct competitors (Omega, Rolex and Zenith). Consequently, the manufacturers of precision watches needed to differentiate themselves through a stronger brand identity, which included design and name. During the 1950s, Longines launched new models of luxury watches that can be considered as a new kind of global product. They had the same sub-brand, design, price and image throughout the world. Yet, it was not so much Longines itself that was rebranded and globalized but rather specific luxury products made by this company and sold with special sub-brands. At the same time, Longines continued to localize products as late as the 1970s and 1980s. The major changes occurred in the 1990s, in relation to the new industrial organization of the Swiss watch industry and its overall shift towards luxury. Longines became part of the Swatch Group at its foundation in 1983 and adopted a new form of brand management in this context.

Moreover, while watch manufacturers launched global collections, the end of state protection on the Swiss watch industry, introduced in the mid-1930s to prevent the relocation of production and technology transfer to other countries, became a challenge for the reputation of the Swiss-made label. Liberalization would allow the relocation in Asia of low value- added activities, such as the production of parts and assembly, abroad.[40] For example, the Société Suisse pour l'Industrie Horlogère SA (SSIH), the holding company that owned Omega, invested in the production of watch components in Hong Kong and Singapore in the 1970s.[41] This new development created a need for discussions on what could and could not be transferred in order to sustain the 'Swiss made' appellation.

One of the first to discuss this issue was a professor in law at the University of Geneva, Edmond Martin-Achard. He gave a public conference in Geneva in November 1958 and published a paper in an academic journal the following year on 'The Swiss Nationality of Watches'.[42] A specialist in intellectual property, he discussed what formed the basis for the Swiss nature of a watch. He concluded that the origin of parts was not important; instead, the place of final assembly was. A watch assembled in Switzerland with foreign parts was Swiss. What mattered was the quality of the product and, for Martin-Achard, assembling a watch in Switzerland would guarantee its high precision.

This opinion was not shared by all the industry, however. Entrepreneurs opposing liberalization, mostly part producers and owners of small family firms without the capital necessary to relocate production abroad, argued that the state-backed cartel already offered protection for watches made completely in Switzerland; to them, then, there was no need to debate the Swiss nature of the watch. A federal report released in March 1959 explained that 'as long as the import [of parts] is, in principle, forbidden, the buyers of Swiss watches are certain to possess a watch entirely produced in Switzerland. The supporters of import restrictions argue that the possibility to use foreign parts and movement-blanks involves by itself a kind of damage to the image of the Swiss watch in the public eye – what they called its "goodwill".'[43] This position was a minority opinion, though, and the gradual end of state protection (which began in 1961) was not accompanied by any legal definition of the Swiss watch. The federal authorities adopted an ordinance on the technical control of watches to ensure that export watches from Switzerland had a minimum quality standard. The control came into force in 1962, but it was loose; thus, it is difficult to evaluate its real effects.[44] This also led the colonial government of Hong Kong to approach the Swiss authorities in 1967 to enquire as to what a 'Swiss made' watch officially was, as government officials wanted to suppress the emergence of fake products and promote a high-tech subcontracting industry.[45]

Discussions continued during the late 1960s and gradually shaped a consensus, which was then legislated in the *Ordinance for the Protection of the Swiss Name of Watches*, adopted in 1971.[46] The law stipulated a number of criteria for 'Swiss made' labelling, the main requirement being that at least half of the value of the components of the movement had to be produced and assembled on Swiss soil. Consequently, half of a movement's parts and all external parts (the case, dial, hands, strap, etc.) could be supplied by foreign plants. This was a very pragmatic measure with a twofold objective: keeping employment in Switzerland and strengthening the competitiveness of Swiss watch companies by allowing the offshoring – mainly in Asia – of low value-added production activities.

As a result, the emergence of global brands was accompanied by the end of state control over the Swiss watch industry and the adoption of a Swiss-made law. This allowed production to be semi-globalized, in the sense that certain activities could be relocated from the 1960s onwards. More than the product itself, its reputation, embodied in a strong brand and an easily identifiable design, ensured its reputation on the world market.

Global luxury brands

The mass production of high-quality mechanical watches and the advent of quartz watches made Japan the world's largest and most competitive nation in the watch industry during the 1970s and the first part of the 1980s. This led to a deep crisis in Switzerland, characterized by the loss of about two-thirds of the employment and the disappearance of numerous firms. However, in the early 1980s, the industrial reorganization realized under the leadership of Nicolas G. Hayek, which gave birth in 1983 to the foundation of the Société Suisse de Microélectronique et d'Horlogerie (SMH, renamed Swatch Group in 1998), and the launch of the Swatch, enabled the Swiss watch industry to recover its dominant position – and to strengthen it over the years until today.[47]

Brand management played an important role in this comeback. The Swatch demonstrated that a watch was not only a useful tool that told the time but a fashion accessory that carried values and that SMH used to tell stories to the public. The identity of the brand was not related to its precision but to an intangible and emotional dimension. Swatch showed the importance of putting an end to the adaptation of local markets – or limiting it drastically. Throughout the world, the products were the same, and they offered a similar message. They were soon distributed in a new retail format that would emphasize this consistency globally: mono-brand stores.[48]

The luxury segment, embodied by the worldwide success of Rolex, followed a similar path. Watches must present a globally unified style and incorporate strong, intangible values. The emergence of global brands in the luxury goods industry is not unique to watchmaking. A similar phenomenon is visible, at the same time, in other luxury sectors.[49] In the 1990s, the management of watch brands underwent profound changes in response to the need to reposition them in this new context. The case of Longines is again emblematic of this move.[50]

Compagnie des Montres Longines was merged into Swatch Group when the latter was established. The restructuring strategy implemented within this group led to the closure of Longines' production workshop in 1988 and its transfer to ETA SA, the subsidiary in charge of movement production for all watch companies of the group. That year, the head of the sales and marketing department, Walter von Känel, was appointed CEO of Longines. From that time on, Longines focused on marketing activities, especially brand management. The aim was to transform the brand – to focus its identity on a few key elements taken from the company's history (classical elegance, technical quality, contribution to sport) and incorporate the so-called values of the firm – and to use it throughout the world with very few adaptations.

Hence, the transformation of the brand occurred in the early 1990s, within the context set out above. It was repositioned in a less expensive segment, which corresponds to what scholars in management call 'accessible luxury',[51] and graphically redesigned as an object of elegance and classicism that did not compete head-on with the Swatch Group's other products situated in the same product range – namely, Rado (high technology and modern design), Glasshütte Original (technical tradition and classicism) and Tissot (modern sports and new technology). Since the 1990s, Longines has refocused on sponsoring activities consistent with this image of classic elegance (horse riding, gymnastics, skiing and tennis), abandoning former areas such as Formula 1 racing (1992). Unlike Blancpain, a company acquired in 1992 that emphasizes the traditional know-how of its watchmaking craftsmen (see Chapter 4), Longines is part of the historical tradition of a manufacture that played a pioneering role in modernizing and industrializing watch production, an image better suited to its 'affordable luxury' products.[52]

This repositioning undertaken in the 1990s featured three main characteristics. First, Swatch Group negotiated an end to licensing contracts, managing to have them cancelled in South Korea (1993) and the United States (1994).[53] From this point on, headquarters controlled the design and style of all Longines watches sold worldwide. Second, Longines strengthened its historical roots via the launch of anniversary models, for example the sub-brands Charleston (1986) and Grande Classique (1992). Moreover, in 1992, the 160th anniversary of the company's founding provided an occasion for opening a brand museum and publishing a corporate history. Third, in 1996, Longines opted for *elegance* as the key concept of the brand and the company. More specifically, it referred to the classical elegance of the interwar years, a period during which Longines used the slogan 'precise and elegant' for its advertising campaigns and which became the source of inspiration for designers in the 1990s and from 2000 onwards. The sub-brand and collection Dolce Vita was launched in 1997 with rectangular models inspired by a watch produced in 1925. This strategy was developed in the years that followed – for example, with the sub-brands Les Elégantes (2002) and Evidenza (2003) (see Figure 3.6).

Conclusion

The brief analysis in this chapter of the historical development of brand management in the Swiss watch industry highlighted two essential elements in the revitalization of brands and the awakening of sleeping beauties.

First, it emphasized the fact that Swiss watchmakers made early and massive use of trademarks and brands. Some of them, albeit a minority, have been signing their watches with their name since at least the eighteenth

Figure 3.6 Advertisement Longines, 2005.

Source: *Europa Star Europe*, no. 270, 2005, p. 17 © Archives Europa Star.

Note: The sub-brand Dolce Vita, launched by Longines in 1997, is an excellent example of the heritage strategy developed by this company during the 1990s. Elegance became the core concept of this brand and was linked to the interwar years.

century. The emergence of a legal framework in 1880 led to the registration of thousands of trademarks right up to the present day. The trademark is thus an essential intangible asset. For today's entrepreneurs, this mass of trademarks also represents an almost inexhaustible potential of sleeping beauties to be awakened.

Second, the history of brand management in the watchmaking industry demonstrates the major disruption embodied by the luxury strategy. This was first observed in the 1940s–1970s for certain models, for which manufacturers developed global sub-brands, and then more systematically from the 1980s onwards. When the watch ceases to be a simple precision instrument and becomes a luxury accessory with great emotional resonance, the brand takes on a new dimension. It becomes part of a new context, that of heritage, built by teams of managers to embody a message and values (see Chapter 1).

Chapter 4

The revival of vanished brands

The first and most widespread way to reawaken sleeping beauties in the watch industry is to relaunch brands that have disappeared. There are many reasons why brands vanish. For example, their owners can go bankrupt or be taken over by a rival firm, they can cease exploiting these brands due to a change of strategy, and a change in the social and political environment can lead to the end of private brands, as in the case of communist countries. Brands are never created forever. One day, most of them become extinct.

In the watch industry, the idea to relaunch vanished brands emerged in the 1980s. The crisis faced by the Swiss watch industry at that time made it necessary to develop new business models to regain competitiveness against the Japanese watchmakers who had established themselves as the new leaders in this industry, thanks to their high-quality and cheap watches.[1] The point was to transform the watch from a precision instrument giving the right time to a luxury fashion accessory that expressed the tradition of the Swiss watchmaking craft. Although there was a general shift towards quartz watches, some major companies in the high-end segment, notably Patek, Philippe & Cie and Montres Rolex SA, kept focused on mechanical watches because it gave sense to their position as the representative of the excellence of Swiss watchmaking. In 1981, Philippe Stern, managing director of Patek Philippe & Cie, explained that he was 'fully convinced that there will be a return to the mechanical watch in the high-end segment, where perfection can be taken to its highest point'.[2] Similarly, although Rolex mastered technology for making quartz watches and produced some in the early 1980s, this product has always remained extremely secondary in its collections.[3]

However, the technical know-how related to mechanical watchmaking was not enough to embody this tradition. Brands needed to build a heritage strategy to offer not only exceptional watches but also a story that accompanied them. At that time, the continuity between the past and the present was a major issue. Buying and relaunching a vanished brand appeared hence as the perfect way to acquire a historical legitimacy to become a representative of the Swiss watchmaking tradition. Blancpain was the first successful case (see case 1). It paved the way for many similar attempts.

During the 1990s, the large industrial groups and luxury conglomerate that dominated the watch industry understood the potential offered by such brands. Reawakening vanished brands was seen as a way to quickly and easily develop new niche markets. These companies had the financial, management and technological resources necessary to carry out such a business on a large scale. However, they were not always successful. The case of Léon Hatot, relaunched by the Swatch Group, demonstrates that a weak heritage strategy can lead to failure (see case 2). Similarly, historic brands from Glashütte, in Germany, had a very different destiny after their takeover by Swatch Group and Richemont (see case 3). Blancpain needs hence to be considered as an exceptionally successful case: in 2022, it was the only reawakened vanished brand that appeared in the top twenty largest Swiss watch brands.[4] The most competitive brands have a certain continuity, although most of them have experienced change of ownership and deep transformation of brand heritage strategy over time (see Chapter 5). However, this does not prevent luxury conglomerates from continuing to invest in the revival of long-established brands. Hence, in 2023, LVMH (Louis Vuitton Moët-Hennessy) announced the intention of its subsidiary Louis Vuitton to relaunch the two brands Gerald Genta and Daniel Roth.[5] These two brands, purchased by Bulgari in 1999, had become the property of LVMH when it acquired the Italian jeweller. They were not, however, exploited. What Louis Vuitton will do with them is still unclear, but they will surely be used to strengthen its legitimacy as a creative watchmaker, after having succeeded in being recognized as a haute couture brand.[6]

Beyond large companies, one must emphasize the impact of crowdfunding and social networks on the rebirth of numerous brands throughout the last fifteen years. New technology has made it possible to relaunch a brand without investing much in marketing and distribution, and outsourcing production. Among Swiss brands, examples include Excelsior Park (a former manufacturer of chronographs based in Saint-Imier that closed down in 1984) or Nivada (a watch manufacturer from Grenchen that formally ceased to exist in 1997).[7] The revival of vanished brands by individual entrepreneurs is often a small-scale business, focused on the development of a few high-quality watches through cooperation with independent suppliers and positioned on a niche market. To date, there is no example of a reawakened sleeping beauty after 2010 that has been able to enter the ranking of the top fifty largest watch brands established yearly by Morgan Stanley.

Finally, one must remember that Switzerland is not the only place where entrepreneurs have taken the opportunity to reawaken sleeping beauties from the watch industry. Watchmaking largely disappeared from the United States and Europe in the context of deindustrialization in the 1970s and 1980s.[8] After 2000, some businessmen tried to relaunch American, French, German and Soviet watch brands that carried a long history – in particular, brands that had once dominated their national market, like Junghans in Germany, Poljot and Raketa in Russia and Chronotechna in Czechia. However, their market shares are extremely low. They target a thin consumer basis made of collectors and fans of the brand.[9]

Case 1: The first mover: Blancpain

The Swiss watch industry faced an existential crisis during the years 1975–85. The oil crisis and the sharp rise in the Swiss franc following the end of the Bretton Woods system highlighted the loss of competitiveness of Swiss watchmaking companies against their Japanese competitors (Seiko, in particular). After the interwar period, Seiko adopted a strategic objective that enabled them to become the world leader in the first part of the 1980s: the mass production of high-precision watches. The switch to quartz strengthened the competitiveness of Japanese firms but was not the cause of it. The industrial reorganization of the Swiss watchmaking industry – carried out under the aegis of the consultant Nicolas G. Hayek and characterized by a series of mergers that gave rise in 1983 to the Société Suisse de Microélectronique et d'Horlogerie (SMH, renamed Swatch Group in 1998) – enabled the Swiss watchmaking industry to regain its competitiveness.[10] The rationalization undertaken by Hayek and the launch of the Swatch were the main driving forces.[11]

The context of this crisis was, however, also an opportunity for the rebirth of the mechanical watch and the foundation of new companies exploiting this product as the expression of the Swiss tradition of watch manufacturing. Reacting against the transformation of the watch industry and the advent of electronic watches mass-produced by giant organizations, several artisan watchmakers worked to recover the authenticity of their craft and to continue manufacturing mechanical watches.[12] Most of them had accumulated experience in the restoration of old watches and clocks in museums and the Antiquorum auction house. They wanted to keep a tradition alive and established themselves as independent watchmakers. This was, for example, the case for Michel Parmigiani (1976), Vincent Calabrese (1977), Philippe Dufour (1978), Roger Dubuis (1980), Franck Müller (1984) and François-Paul Journe (1985).[13] Although these artisan watchmakers were attached to a manufacturing tradition (mechanical watches), they had no interest in relaunching old, declining or extinguished brands. Some of them also registered old brands with a strong potential for a relaunch but never exploited them. For example, Michel Parmigiani registered Bovet Fleurier (1989) and Juvet Fleurier (1991), but he focused on his own name and sold the aforementioned brands to other investors.[14] Independent watchmakers wanted to develop and produce watches under their own name, with their own style and their own originality. However, they showed that the market for high-value mechanical watches was not dead.

Moreover, at the same time, a new generation of watch companies based on a clear marketing objective emerged in Geneva. Some entrepreneurs with extensive experience in sales used their knowledge of what consumers wanted to buy to launch new brands, such as Robergé Watches (1972) and Raymond Weil (1976).[15] This contributed to making Geneva the new centre of the Swiss watch industry.

Figure 4.1 Advertisement for Blancpain, 1957.

Source: *The Eastern Jeweller and Watchmaker*, no. 39, 1957 © Archives Europa Star.

Note: Rayville SA was a small company specializing in ladies watches. Although it used 1735 as its foundation year in its advertisement, it was not a part of a heritage strategy. This advertisement shows clearly that neither the product nor the message were inserted in a general narrative that stresses the tradition of Swiss watchmaking. The presence of the doll is a reference to the past, but the link with the modern product is not emphasized.

In this context, Blancpain SA was founded in the early 1980s to revive the same name brand, which had gradually disappeared from the market since the 1960s. Blancpain was the name of the family which had owned a small watch manufacturer in Villeret, a village close to Saint-Imier, in Bernese Jura. However, during the 1950s, this firm, which had been renamed Rayville SA in 1933, faced a challenge experienced by many family watch companies at that time: its annual output amounted at about 100,000 watches in a broad range of models (see Figure 4.1).[16] It was thus impossible to rationalize production and remain competitive on the global market, where the pressure by large companies required a change. In 1961, Rayville SA, employing some 200 workers, reached an agreement with Société Suisse pour l'industrie horlogère (SSIH), the largest watchmaking group in Switzerland, which already owned Omega, Tissot, Lemania and Marc Favre.[17] SSIH took a stake in Rayville SA, making it a subsidiary of the group.[18] Although the company was legally kept alive, it focused on the production of small-calibre jewellery watches for Omega, this product being one of Rayville's specialities after the Second World War. The company continued its existence as a subsidiary of SSIH until it was officially merged by Omega SA in 1980.[19] However, the use of the brand Blancpain was gradually abandoned by SSIH, which became part of SMH in 1983.

In the meantime, the Blancpain brand was purchased in 1982 by Frédéric Piguet SA, a manufacturer of complicated mechanical watch movements, for a sum of about 20,000 francs.[20] The following year, a new company, Blancpain SA, was founded in Le Chenit, in Vallée de Joux. It was a startup with a small capital (50,000 francs) and the financial support of Credit Suisse.[21] The board of directors included three people: Jacques Piguet, president, as well as Jean-Claude Biver and Michel Favre, secretary.[22] This company then in 1984 became the owner of the Blancpain brand.[23] Jacques Piguet, a graduate in engineering, had in 1978 become the fourth-generation owner and director of a family firm founded in 1858 and specialized in the production of mechanical ebauches and movements for high-quality and complicated watches.[24] It had a production of about 250,000 pieces in the mid-1980s and supplied renowned brands, such as Audemars Piguet and Cartier.[25] As for Jean-Claude Biver, he had entered Audemars Piguet in 1975, after his studies in business at HEC Lausanne, and then moved to Omega in 1980.[26] He resigned from Omega in 1982, became director of a textile company that bankrupted in 1983, and joined Piguet to relaunch Blancpain.[27]

The original idea of Biver and Piguet was to launch a brand of exclusive luxury mechanical watches. Frédéric Piguet SA could provide the movements, and Blancpain was the perfect name for such a project. As this brand had nearly not been used in the 1960s and 1970s, no quartz watch bearing this name had ever been marketed. The brand was 'pure' of any modern technology. Moreover, and foremost, archival documents showed that Blancpain family activity in watchmaking could be traced back to 1735. This made it the oldest watch manufacturer in the world, and Biver was keen to exploit this idea.

Indeed, historical research in public archives commissioned by Jean-Jacques Fiechter, the last director of Rayville SA, has shown that Jehan Jacques Blancpain, in Villeret, was mentioned as a watchmaker in a property cadastre dated 1735. This is the oldest known mention of a Blancpain watchmaker.[28] He would have worked on the second floor of the family farm, where he would have established a small workshop in the middle of the eighteenth century. It is true that the village of Villeret and all the upper valley of Saint-Imier was a place where watchmaking emerged in Switzerland at that time. Jehan Jacques' descendants pursued and developed this business throughout the nineteenth century, gradually modernizing the mode of production but keeping a small dimension and family ownership. During the first third of the twentieth century, the Blancpain manufacturer produced a broad range of watches, particularly small watches for ladies and complicated watches. In 1932, when Frédéric-Emile Blancpain, a representative of the seventh generation at the head of the family firm, passed away, his children did not want to continue this business. In light of this, it was taken over the next year by its two managers, Betty Fiechter and André Léal, under the name Rayville SA.[29] The company enjoyed some success after the war, particularly with small jewellery watches and a diving watch launched in 1953, the Fifty Fathom model.

It was not the whole story of this company that interested Biver in the early 1980s but merely the fact that one could argue it was the oldest watch manufacturer. The main asset of the brand was the year – 1735 – attached to its name. Hence, the strategy adopted by Biver, called by a Swiss newspaper a 'seller of nostalgia',[30] went against the grain of the industry as a whole. Rejecting quartz, he built the image of a brand based on tradition and technical excellence, the foundations of the company's upmarket positioning. The new headquarters were not established in the village of Villeret. Given that it was far from Geneva and the Bernese Jura, and experiencing a deep industrial crisis, it was not a glamourous place for a story stressing the excellence of the watchmaking tradition.[31] Instead, the founders of Blancpain SA chose Le Brassus, a village in the Vallée de Joux, which is the historical heart of the production of highly complicated Swiss watches. This location, in a region that represented watchmaking excellence and where such companies as Audemars Piguet and Jaeger LeCoultre had been present since their founding in the nineteenth century, reinforced Blancpain's technical legitimacy. It was also close enough to Geneva and Cointrin airport to easily bring wealthy customers and journalists.

Moreover, in declaring 1735 as its foundation year and advertising its watches as 'made in the tradition of eighteenth-century master watchmakers', Blancpain proclaimed itself 'the oldest watch brand in the world'.[32] The first watches developed by Blancpain SA, using Frédéric Piguet SA's manufacturing capabilities, were mostly mechanical watches with complications like moon phases, perpetual calendars, tourbillons or erotic figures. The style was extremely classic, in order to emphasize the tribute to tradition (see Figure 4.2).

The strategy worked, and Blancpain SA enjoyed rapid success. It organized a distribution system based on the principles of the luxury business: sales through an exclusive network of specialized retailers throughout the world, limited volumes and high unit prices. The company's turnover rose sharply from 4.9 million francs in 1984 to around 60 million in 1991.[33] Blancpain had a bright future; the potential for growth seemed unlimited. It required, however, the investment of more capital to develop the production system and a worldwide retail presence. In the early 1990s, following the foundation of Moët-Hennessy Louis Vuitton (LVMH) and of Compagnie Financière Richemont, the luxury industry had entered a phase of consolidation.[34] Louis Vuitton and other investors would have approached Blancpain SA.[35] Finally, Piguet and Biver decided to sell their two companies, Frédéric Piguet SA and Blancpain SA, to SMH for an amount estimated to be between 60 and 80 million francs.[36] This takeover enabled Hayek to acquire an exclusive luxury brand to complete his portfolio. He also took control of one of the very rare manufacturers of high-end mechanical movements and could, from this moment, produce in-house any kind of watch, from the simplest to the most complicated. Moreover, SMH could internalize the genius marketing flair of Biver. Beyond personal profit from this sale, Biver was offered a position within SMH. He was still the managing director of Blancpain and took charge of repositioning Omega in the accessible luxury segment, an operation once again crowned with success.[37]

The first years within SMH had no real impact on the product development and heritage strategy of Blancpain. The brand continued to focus on the expression of the Swiss watchmaking tradition. The message of the brand and the design of its watches remained the same. Then, in the middle of the 1990s, there was a move towards the creation of a second collection of sporty watches – the demand for luxury sports watches was soaring, as expressed by the growing demand for Audemars Piguet's Royal Oak.[38] Blancpain was able to enter this market with the relaunch of a model developed in 1953: the diving watch Fifty Fathoms. It had encountered short-term success in the 1950s but had basically disappeared after the early 1970s. In 1997, Blancpain SA relaunched this model, which was presented to the public as the embodiment of the long-term involvement of the brand for innovation in watchmaking. Tradition and diving watches are still today the two major pillars of Blancpain (see Figure 4.3).

After 2000, Blancpain experienced a deep transformation within Swatch Group (as SMH was renamed in 1998). First, there was a major change in terms of management. Marc A. Hayek, grandson of Nicolas, was appointed marketing manager (2001), and then managing director of Blancpain at the age of thirty-two (2003). Such a fast promotion had undoubtedly something to do with Jean-Claude Biver's departure from the Swatch Group (2003).[39] Marc Hayek also joined Swatch Group's extended management board (2002), then the executive group management board (2005).[40] Consequently, when Nicolas G. Hayek died in 2010, there was no break in

The Revival of Vanished Brands

Figure 4.2 Advertisement for Blancpain, 1994.

Source: *Europa Star China*, no. 33, 1994 © Archives Europa Star.

Note: The campaign developed by Biver for Blancpain focuses on the exploitation of a heritage: the watch itself has a traditional design and complications, while the slogan claims the will to keep tradition alive.

Figure 4.3 Advertisement for Blancpain, 2010.

Source: *Europa Star Russia*, no. 23, 2010 © Archives Europa Star.

Note: Besides watches embodying the tradition of Swiss watchmaking, Blancpain holds a collection of sports watches called Fifty Fathoms. It can be considered in itself as the reawakening of the brand. Despite its more modern design, this model is not used to target a lower price segment but to compete directly with similar products made by rival brands like Rolex (Submariner) and Omega (Seamaster).

governance, with his daughter Nayla becoming chairman of the board and his son, Nick, remaining chairman of the executive board. Marc, the son of Nayla, remained the head of Blancpain and extended his direction over other luxury brands of the group.

The most important change under the leadership of Marc Hayek is not related to product development or heritage strategy, which basically continued what had been set up in the 1980s and 1990s. A major transformation occurred regarding the production facilities.[41] At the end of the 2000s, there was a real consolidation of manufacturing for top-of-the-range timepieces, as Swatch Group needed to secure the means to grow its sales volume in this segment. In 2008, Blancpain SA announced the takeover of Vica SA, the company founded by Vincent Calabrese, a watchmaking artisan who had developed grand complication watches such as tourbillons for Blancpain in the 1980s.[42] Two years later, in 2010, the production of high-end movements was reorganized. Frédéric Piguet SA was taken over by its main customer, Blancpain SA. The same went for Valdar SA, a producer of watch components acquired by Swatch Group together with Breguet (see Chapter 6), which was merged by François Golay SA, a manufacturer of wheels purchased by Frédéric Piguet SA two years earlier. This twofold restructuring strengthened Blancpain's production capacity by verticalizing the manufacture, on the one hand, and rationalizing the production of high-end components, on the other.

The maintenance of the heritage strategy built by Biver and the restructuring of the production system after 2000 offered excellent conditions for growth. According to the estimates of investment bankers, the gross sales of Blancpain went from 115 million francs in 2006 to 150 million francs in 2010 and 420 million in 2022.[43] Blancpain was ranked the nineteenth largest Swiss watch brand in 2022, just before Chopard, Swatch and Bulgari.[44]

Case 2: The failed reawakening of Léon Hatot

During the second part of the 1990s, the takeover of Blancpain and the relaunch of Omega had shown Nicolas G. Hayek that high-value-added watches, rather than watch movements and components, offered a unique opportunity for expansion in the fast-increasing luxury market.[45] There was, however, a need to hold a full-set portfolio of brands positioned in various complementary segments. The acquisition of brands and companies enabled Swatch Group to build such a portfolio in 1999–2001. Hayek purchased Breguet, Léon Hatot, Jaquet Droz and Glashütte Uhrentriebe from various investors.[46] He positioned each of these brands on a specific niche market.

Léon Hatot had a particular importance: it offered ladies' jewellery watches, a segment with growing popularity in the late 1990s and a scene from which Swatch Group was nearly completely absent at that time. The acquisition of a series of jewels, watches and drawings having belonged to Léon Hatot, auctioned by Christie's in Geneva in 1989, was the opportunity to get hold of a brand that could be used for the development of jewellery watches.[47] How Swatch Group was able to purchase this collection is unclear. However, in September 1994, Omega SA applied for the registration of the Léon Hatot brand in France.[48] It took a few more years before a business model suitable for the use of this watch was developed. Although he hardly mentioned publicly his role at the head of this brand, probably due to its failure, Jean-Claude Biver played an important role. He was in charge of the management of Léon Hatot brand before the creation of a specific company in 2001.[49] Relaunching this brand was hence probably based on a concept similar to the one that had made Blancpain a success story.

Léon Hatot was a French watchmaker of the first part of the twentieth century.[50] Born in 1883, he graduated from the Watchmaking School of Besançon and in 1905 opened in this city a small workshop specializing in watchcase engraving. It was a small business employing around twelve people. In 1911, while keeping his engraving workshop in Besançon, Hatot took over Maison Bredillard, a small company based in Paris, and engaged in the development of artistic watches and clocks. In 1926, he entrusted the management of the Parisian company to his son-in-law, Edouard Dietsch.[51] Two years later, the company and its store moved from Rue de la Paix to the famous Faubourg Saint-Honoré, closer to its wealthy customers.[52] During the interwar years, the Parisian workshop marketed its own goods and supplied well-renowned jewellers, such as Boucheron and Cartier.[53] At the same time, in Besançon, Hatot started to carry out intense research and development in two main fields: automatic watches and, especially, electrical clocks. He applied for two patents, for a watch case and a watch strap, in March 1912. Until his death, his company received 102 more patents, essentially related to electric clocks.[54] The production and sales of electrical clocks and instruments was realized by a subsidiary founded in Besançon in 1920. He launched a specific brand, ATO, for his electrical clocks, in 1923. After his

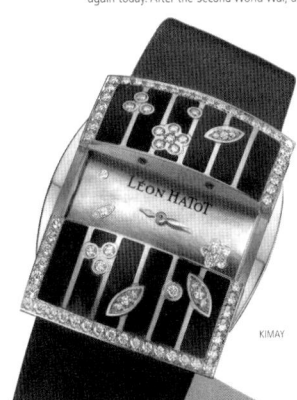

Figure 4.4 Presentation of the relaunch of Léon Hatot in *Europa Star*, 2004.

Source: *Europa Star Europe*, no. 267, 2004 (c) Archives Europa Star.

Note: The original position of a jewellery brand as a tribute to Art Deco is embodied by the creation of a model (bottom left) inspired by the drawing of Léon Hatot acquired at an auction (top left).

death, in 1953, Léon Hatot's company was pursued, but it faced severe financial difficulties. Hence, it had to sell its patents to other firms specializing in electrical clocks and refocused on various instruments and display panels.[55]

The history of Léon Hatot was thus broad and diversified. He had been an entrepreneur with many varied interests, from technological innovation to art and luxury. Swatch Group decided to focus on the activities of the Parisian company to build a heritage based on Art Deco and jewellery. A new firm, Léon Hatot SA, was registered in Neuchâtel in 2001, with a capital of 100,000 francs. The board of directors consisted of Nicolas G. Hayek, president, his son Nick, and two managers of Swatch Group, Edgar Geiser (finances) and Hanspeter Rentsch (legal affairs). Arlette-Elsa Emch was appointed executive director.[56] She was in charge of launching the new jewellery watch.

Emch had joined Swatch Group in 1992 as a communication manager, before being appointed president of CK Watch in 1997, the subsidiary that was producing and selling watches under licence for the US designer Calvin Klein. She led Swatch Group to embark on the development of jewellery collections for its various brands and became the head of a new company founded for this purpose in 2000, Dress Your Body (DYB).[57] For Léon Hatot, she wanted a new watch and jewellery brand – one that was 'entirely and extremely feminine'.[58] Swatch Group claimed in 2004 that Léon Hatot was 'the one and only top-class jewelry brand exclusively dedicated to women'.[59]

The objective was to launch jewellery watches inspired by Art Deco and build a heritage on the 5000 drawings acquired from Christie's auction. According to Emch, 'these sketches and drawings testify to the values of an era when these creations glorified femininity'.[60] A first series of watches and jewellery was presented to the public in 2004 (see Figure 4.4). Together with a few unique or small-series pieces, Léon Hatot SA launched five collections of jewellery watches: Zelia (architectural model with pure lines), Luela (inspiration from Indian printed fabrics), Aimay (softness and curves), Kimay (inspiration from Japan) and Mae (floral patterns).[61] For a few years, the company continued to develop both highly priced artistic jewellery to strengthen the fame of the brand and jewellery watches manufactured in larger series. For example, in 2007, Hatot launched the Jazzy necklace, valued at 750,000 francs, as a tribute to 'Art Deco years, to Josephine Baker, to the volutes of cigars, to rhythm, to freedom'.[62] The original target of the brand was the exclusive luxury segment, with entry-level prices at 5900 francs and an average price of 15,000 francs.[63]

Several actions were quickly taken to establish the Léon Hatot brand as a legitimate representative of fine jewellery and watchmaking. In 2005, a coffee-table book was published by Assouline under the name of Arlette-Elsa Emch.[64] The same year, a private exhibition was organized for selected customers at Christie's showroom in Paris.[65] Moreover, again in 2005, Léon Hatot recruited its first ambassador: Opera de Paris ballet star Marie-Agnes Gillot. She was followed in 2006 by Lebanese singer Nelly Makdessy. Finally, the brand had its first stand at Baselworld in 2006.

At the same time, Léon Hatot started to develop its own retail network, a necessary condition for success in the exclusive segment. Its watches were offered in the Tourbillons Boutiques, the network of multi-brand stores launched in 2001 by Swatch Group for its own luxury brands, as well as in some independent multi-brand retailers. It also opened its own mono-brand stores in famous places for luxury shopping, starting with Paris (2003), followed by Cannes (2004), Geneva (2005), Nice (2006), Courchevel (2006), Taiwan (2006), Tokyo (2007) and again Paris, at Place Vendôme (2007).[66] The management of this retail network was realized by a second company founded in 2006 in Bienne with a capital of 100,000 francs, Léon Hatot Les Boutiques SA. Arlette-Elsa Emch was appointed president and managing director.[67]

However, despite its entry onto the Chinese market in 2007, success was hard to achieve in the highly competitive market of jewellery watches. In 2006, the brokerage company Helvea estimated the gross sales of Léon Hatot to be a mere five million francs.[68] It was very far from that of established jewellery watch brands, for which sales that year were estimated to be at 284 million for Piaget, 409 million for Chopard and 457 million for Bulgari.[69] Léon Hatot tried to improve its competitiveness by decreasing its prices and moving down to the accessible luxury segment. In 2007, Emch explained in the Swiss press that entry-level prices were now at 2,500 francs and that the company was working on the launch of products for 1,500 francs.[70] Simpler watches with a smaller number of jewels appeared in 2008, like the Heartbreaker, which built on the growing popularity of mechanical watches for women (see Figure 4.5). There was, however, an important break with the primary message of Art Deco inspiration.

In 2009, Swatch Group announced a sudden reorganization of the retail network, with most of the mono-brand stores around the world being closed: Léon Hatot watches 'will now be available exclusively in the Leon Hatot flagship boutique in the heart of Geneva, as well as in the high level chain of Swatch Group Tourbillon stores in premium locations around the world'.[71] Moreover, product development underwent a major change, with the company explaining that 'a new collection particularly orientated towards European and Swiss tastes is under preparation'.[72]

However, this collection never appeared. Jewellery was not selling well enough, and the brand Léon Hatot was put on standby in 2009.[73] Arlette-Elsa Emch resigned from her positions at Léon Hatot SA and Léon Hatot Les Boutiques SA. Nick Hayek replaced her on a temporary basis, before handing over the reins in 2010 to his sister, Nayla.[74] Emch, who had also given up the management of DYB in 2010, announced in 2012 her departure from Swatch Group.[75]

During its six years of operations, between 2004 and 2009, Léon Hatot was unable to establish a competitive business model. Swatch Group also looked at other opportunities to engage in the luxury jewellery watch segment. In 2007, it had signed an agreement with Tiffany for the production of watches under licence. However, some disagreements led to the end of cooperation in 2011.[76] Two years

Figure 4.5 New Léon Hatot watch presented to the public in 2008.

Source: *Europa Star Europe*, no. 289, 2008 (c) Archives Europa Star.

Note: The models developed in 2008 to target a more accessible customer basis presented a major aesthetical rupture with the heritage built a few years before. The link with Art Deco disappeared.

later, in 2013, Swatch Group purchased Harry Winston.[77] Cooperating with or taking over a jewellery brand already well established on the market was seen as more effective than building a new brand from scratch. Léon Hatot SA stopped operations and was merged by Omega SA, another company of Swatch Group, in 2013.[78] The following year, Léon Hatot Les Boutiques SA was written off, and its assets were taken over by Omega SA.[79] The brand Léon Hatot still belongs to Swatch Group, but it is not exploited any longer.

How can the failure of Léon Hatot's reawakening be explained? Swiss newspapers argued that the global financial crisis had a negative impact on the sales of jewellery.[80] However, crisis had a very limited impact on Swatch Group: the gross sales of all the company declined by 11 per cent in 2009 but hit a new record the following year, and the operating profit still amounted to more than 900 million francs in 2009.[81] Moreover, some jewellery watches, like Piaget, resisted well.[82] The crisis is hence not a sufficient reason to explain the failure of Léon Hatot. Two other factors played a major role.

First, one must consider the specificity of the jewellery watch segment. It is a very conservative business in which only very few new brands had been able to establish a competitive position over the last decades. The jewellery industry is indeed characterized by the existence of numerous small local brands and a handful of global brands that dominate the global market.[83] Most jewellery watch brands emerged from a diversification process towards watches by these jewellery companies (Bulgari, Cartier, Harry Winston, Tiffany and Van Cleef & Arpels). The only two successful cases of new entrants from watchmaking were Chopard, which built on the experience of the Scheufele, a German family of jewellers (see Chapter 5), and Piaget, the latter having built a competitive model in the 1960s based on its cooperation with Geneva-based jewellers and the association with celebrities.[84] This context made it very difficult to launch a new brand like Léon Hatot from scratch.

Second, the heritage strategy of Léon Hatot presents major weaknesses. It was developed on a very specific and thin basis: Art Deco jewellery from Paris. Although it gave a clear identity to the first watches marketed in 2004, the message of the brand lacked emotional value transmitted to the public through storytelling. While its competitors emphasized universal emotions, like love or the beauty of nature, and communicated about celebrities attached to their brand, Léon Hatot kept focused on the aesthetic value of its products. It had undoubtedly limited the capacity to create strong emotional bonds with the public and consumers.

Case 3: German brands from Glashütte

Not all watch brands disappeared because their owners focused on other businesses and gradually stopped using them. Major political disruptions, like the advent of communism and the nationalization of private firms, also played an important role, particularly in the USSR and Eastern Europe. After the fall of the Berlin Wall, some entrepreneurs took the opportunity to reawaken brands that had vanished with state ownership. The German watch industry is an excellent case in point. Although it had never been wholly concentrated in eastern Germany – there were actually numerous large firms throughout the national territory – the tradition of high-quality watchmaking had been clustered in a small town in Saxony, Glashütte. This therefore offered the best potential to relaunch brands after 1989.[85]

Even though Germany had a long tradition of clockmaking in the Black Forest, as well as in some cities like Dresden, Leipzig and Nuremberg, where Peter Henlein (1479–1542) would have invented the world's first watch,[86] the birthplace of the German watch industry was a small town in Saxony, close to the current border with the Czech Republic, Glashütte. Ferdinand Adolph Lange, a graduate of the Technical College in Dresden who benefited from training in Switzerland and France, founded his own company in Glashütte in 1845 with a particular aim: to produce quality watches in order to compete with the Swiss watchmakers who at that time dominated the German market.[87] Although the mass production of clocks and watches was founded in 1864 in Schramberg, in the Black Forest, by Grebrüder Junghans, Lange distinguished itself with the quality of its products. The firm, taken over by the second generation in 1875 under the name A. Lange & Söhne, remained a small business until the beginning of the twentieth century. Its production amounted to a mere 1,500 pocket watches in 1891, and it had a workforce of only 250 employees in 1900.[88]

A twofold organizational structure characterized the German watch industry during the first part of the twentieth century: large industrial enterprises, Junghans being the most important, and a broad range of small, specialized companies, among which were A. Lange & Söhne and other small firms that had flourished in Glashütte. After 1945, this industry underwent a major reorganization, marked not only by the reconstruction of companies after the end of the war but also by the deep division between western Germany (German Federal Republic) and eastern Germany (German Democratic Republic). In the west, the watch industry experienced a boom until the quartz revolution. Companies like the ebauches factory Durowe AG, as well as Junghans, established themselves as leading competitors on the world market.

As for the eastern German watch industry, concentrated in Glashütte, it endured a profound industrial transformation following the establishment of a communist regime. All the watch companies in this city, including A. Lange & Söhne, were merged in 1951 into a state-owned conglomerate: VEB Glashütter Uhrentriebe (GUB). In 1967, it merged with another state-owned watch manufacturer, Ruhla.[89] Both companies possessed automated production technologies and set up a system for the mass production of standardized products. Their production volume amounted to approximately 2.2 million watches, which were mainly sold on the domestic market, in other Eastern European countries and in the USSR.[90]

In the 1980s, the crisis caused by the rise of Asian watchmakers affected German watch companies in the same way as Swiss firms. Junghans, the large company that had traditionally dominated the watch industry in West Germany, experienced a significant decline during the 1980s. Its watch turnover fell from 320 million marks in 1981 to 140 million in 1988.[91] Despite investments in the modernization of the production system and the introduction of quartz watches, the company was unable to survive in the context of a global market that had become extremely competitive. The company was gradually dismantled during the 1990s, and the Junghans brand was sold in 2000 to Egana Goldpfeil, a mid-range fashion goods distribution company founded in Hong Kong in 1978 by a German entrepreneur and specializing in the licensed manufacture of accessories – including watches.[92]

However, as in Switzerland, moving to luxury was the strategy that made possible a comeback of the German watchmaking industry on world markets. Glashütte played a major role in this process because it had been the home of the tradition of craft and excellence since the middle of the nineteenth century. The end of the communist regime and the privatization of state-owned companies presented an opportunity to launch new businesses exploiting the heritage of old famous brands. Two main enterprises thus emerged in the 1990s: A. Lange & Söhne and Glashütte Original.

The first one, A. Lange & Söhne, was still a family firm when it was nationalized after the end of the Second World War. Consequently, in 1990, Walter Lange, the great-grandson of Ferdinand A. Lange, founded a new company, Lange Uhren GmbH, and registered the brand A. Lange & Söhne.[93] He was the owner of the company before its integration into GUB in 1948, and he wanted to relaunch traditional mechanical watches. It was, however, necessary to acquire know-how and manufacturing facilities to develop and produce traditional mechanical watches. The collaboration with IWC International Watch Co., a manufacturer based in Switzerland which belonged at that time to the German industrial conglomerate Mannesmann, made it possible, and IWC received 10 per cent of Lange Uhren's capital. In 1991, Mannesmann founded a new company, Les Manufactures Horlogères (LMH), to manage its business in the watch industry.[94] It owned controlling interests in IWC, Jaeger-LeCoultre and Lange Uhren. The takeover of LMH by Compagnie Financière Richemont in 2000 led to the integration of the brand A. Lange & Söhne into this Swiss-based group.[95] Richemont was already strongly positioned in jewellery watches, with Cartier and Piaget. It had taken over Vacheron Constantin in 1996 and wanted to expand its position in the segment of luxury traditional watches.[96] Entering Richemont allowed Lange Uhren to access the resources of a luxury conglomerate.

It was, for example, possible to use its retail network and to access the US market in 2002.[97]

Product development, however, was the field in which the cooperation with Swiss firms was the most important. Günter Blümlein, CEO of LMH, launched a project in the mid-1990s to develop a grand complication tourbillon wristwatch to show the ambitions of A. Lange & Söhne and establish its legitimacy. The small size and limited resources of this company required cooperation with the Swiss company Renaud & Papi, a small firm founded in 1986 in La Chaux-de-Fonds to develop complicated watch movements.[98] This enabled A. Lange & Söhne to launch in 2006 the world's first one-minute tourbillon in a wristwatch format featuring a fusée-and-chain transmission combined with a chronograph with rattrapante functions (Figure 4.6).[99] Although knowledge rooted in the core of the Swiss watch region was at the origin of the realization of such a watch, it was marketed as a symbol of the excellence of the German watchmaking tradition and the expression of the *Made in Germany*. The takeover by Richemont strengthened the cooperation with Swiss watchmakers to develop similar projects. Being a part of Richemont had finally had a positive impact on sales. A. Lange & Söhne experienced nearly 68 per cent growth of its gross sales between 2012 (145 million francs) and 2022 (243 million francs).[100] This was far higher than the general trend of Swiss watch export at that time (+16 per cent). The success of this brand is undoubtedly linked to the development of highly complicated watches for the exclusive luxury segment. According to Morgan Stanley Research, in 2022, the average retail price of A. Lange & Söhne watches (44,266 francs) made it the fifth most expensive brand, after Richard Mille, Jacob & Co., Van Cleef & Arpels and Audemars Piguet.[101]

The second major brand that emerged in Glashütte in the 1990s was Glashütte Original. In 1994, the state-owned conglomerate GUB was purchased by two German businessmen, Heinz W. Pfeifer, who had a majority stake and became the managing director, and Alfred Wallner, a jeweller from Nuremberg.[102] Unlike Walter Lange, who had again started his business with only a company name and a brand, Pfeifer acquired a manufacturer with production facilities and a full set of assets. However, his idea was to completely change the type of watches he would make. While GUB was focused on the mass production of simple, cheap and standardized watches, Pfeifer had in mind to refocus on luxury and to develop products that embodied the old tradition of watchmaking craft in Saxony. The company was renamed Glashütter Uhrentrieb, and it launched mechanical watches presented as the heirs of a historical tradition.[103] In 1995, Glashütte Original presented a tourbillon watch with a perpetual calendar, priced at 290,000 marks.[104] The German traditional craft was alive, personified by this new brand. At the same time, in 1996, Pfeiffer launched a second brand to target the mass market and keep his main brand focused on exclusive luxury. Union Glashütte was used for cheaper watches, made with ETA movements.[105]

The Revival of Vanished Brands 69

Figure 4.6 Tourbillon watch developed by Lange & Söhne, 2006.
Source: Swisstime, 2006 © Archives Europa Star.
Note: The cooperation with the Swiss manufacturer of complication movements, Renaud & Papi, contributed to re-establish Lange & Söhne as a brand that supported the rebirth of the German watchmaking tradition.

In 2000, Heinz W. Pfeifer sold his company to Swatch Group. He was appointed a member of the extended management board and kept this position until 2004.[106] During these years of transition, Glashütte Original and Union Glashütte were gradually integrated within the Swiss group and benefited from its resources. This made possible an increase of investments in the development of the factory, access to a global network of retailers and the internalization of new marketing knowledge. Moreover, Glashütte Original secured the access of watch components necessary to manufacture in-house complicated mechanical watches (see Figure 4.7).[107]

Despite the integration within Swatch Group, Glashütte Original was not able to benefit from the strong upward trend in sales of luxury watches and was thus unable to enter a phase of fast development. According to estimates by investment banks, its sales amounted to only 60 million francs in 2006 – about half of those by Blancpain.[108] The value of gross sales grew only slightly over last decade, reaching 65 million in 2010 and 85 million in 2015.[109] In 2019, it was back to 60 million, and it did not enjoy

Figure 4.7 Glashütte Original watch launched in 2002.

Source: Swisstime, 2002 © Archives Europa Star.

Note: Although Glashütte Original benefited from the technical know-how of Swatch Group, it remains unclear how and where this product has been designed and produced. Its dial claims it is 'Made in Germany', but this designation is not protected by a law, unlike 'Swiss Made'.

the post-Covid-19 surge of luxury consumption (53 million in 2022).[110] This lack of competitiveness is related to its position in a competitive segment dominated by watches with a strong heritage that includes glamour and emotional value, beyond technical excellence. Unlike A. Lange & Söhne, which is presented as exclusive luxury, Glashütte Original watches are positioned as accessible luxury. Their average retail price in 2022 was 5,186 francs.[111] They are in direct competition with Cartier and Omega, which have dominated this segment since the 1990s.

Glashütte Original was thus a major concern for Swatch Group. The excellence of German traditional watchmaking craft was not a heritage strong enough to achieve long-term development on the global market. In 2008, it tried to use the cheaper brand Union Glashütte to target the mass market. Until this time, the brand had not been

The Revival of Vanished Brands

mentioned in Swatch Group's annual reports. François Thiebaud, CEO of Tissot and in charge of the mid-range brands Certina and Mido, was entrusted with the launch of Union Glashütte. The first targets were Germany and Austria.[112] It expanded later to the whole world. It remained, however, a very small brand, with sales estimated at 15 million francs in 2010 and 2017.[113] According to Morgan Stanley Research, in 2021, it had a 0.1 per cent share of the world watch market, similar to the Flik Flak brand of plastic watches for children.[114]

Conclusion

The various case studies of the reawakening of sleeping beauties analysed in this chapter highlight the fundamental importance of heritage and resources. The important thing is not to discover a brand with a heroic past. The example of Blancpain, which was a first mover in the revival of sleeping beauties and one of the most successful cases, demonstrates that it is possible to build a strong brand without an extraordinary history. For several centuries, Blancpain did not really stand out for its innovations or its products. At best, it was a small watch manufacturer among dozens, if not hundreds. Much more than the history itself, it is the heritage that counts. Biver fully understood the potential of exploiting a brand whose origins date back to 1735 to make it the representative of the Swiss watchmaking tradition. The consistency of the heritage is essential, because it is the foundation on which the emotional values attached to the brand are transmitted. The products are expressions of this heritage. From this point of view, it is interesting to look at failures, because they teach us as much as successes. For example, while Léon Hatot seemed to be developed on the basis of a coherent heritage strategy when it was launched, the fundamental change of direction in 2008 represented a break in terms of the legibility of the heritage. While the brand continued to design products with remarkable style, this was no longer an expression of the brand's emotional values. Consequently, it lost its consumers. Similarly, the example of the many small companies created over the last fifteen years from the revival of a brand underlines the need to weave a link between the brand's past, even if largely imaginary, and the products launched in its honour. The limited resources of these small companies no doubt lead them to pay close attention to the significance of some of the models they develop.

Resources are precisely what enable entrepreneurs who want to relaunch defunct brands to realize their plans. It is not just a question of capital but also of access to expertise in the design and production of complicated watches and jewellery. This is why Biver did not create Blancpain alone; instead, he did it in collaboration with Piguet. Being part of a large company, such as Swatch Group or Richemont, makes it easier to access resources, because they have a wide range of skills in-house, which they put at the service of their various brands. However, it is also possible to have access to production resources if you are an independent company. Several of the examples discussed in this chapter reveal the decisive role played by the watchmaking ecosystem in relaunching brands. Manufacturers such as Renaud & Papi (now part of Audemars Piguet) and Chronode, as well as independent designers, have been instrumental in supporting these projects.

Chapter 5

Brand revival and the recovery of declining firms

Not all sleeping beauties are brands that had vanished from the market because their owners had disappeared or due to an institutional change. The second pattern explored in this chapter focuses on brands that had been unable to establish or keep their competitive advantage and their profitability, or that faced insurmountable difficulties during a period of crisis. A change of ownership and of management can lead such brands to a successful comeback. There are essentially two main reasons why investors acquire declining firms.

First, some managers believe they can implement a better strategy and make the brand competitive. One of the best examples is probably Cartier.[1] This French jeweller, which owned three boutiques – Paris, London and New York – had, since the mid-nineteenth century, presented itself as a manufacturer of exclusive classical jewels for the aristocracy and the happy few. However, the business model was no longer profitable in the 1960s, as it did not meet the expectations of new generations of wealthy classes. The brand did, however, have the potential to develop a story based on the exploitation of a heritage made of iconic products (e.g. Trinity wedding rings and Tank watches), universal values (love and adventure), historical figures (designer Jeanne Toussaint, a friend of Coco Chanel) and symbols (the panther). French businessmen Joseph Kanoui and Alain-Domonique Perrin understood this when they took over the business in 1972. The following year, they launched the concept 'Must de Cartier' and marketed a broad range of accessories, such as lighters and watches, targeting the accessible luxury market. The success was phenomenal, and the brand was sold in 1988 to Compagnie Financière Richemont.

Breitling is another example of success in the watch industry. This company, founded in 1884, specialized in the production of chronographs but was one of the numerous victims of competition from Japan in the 1970s. Its too many models made it impossible to control manufacturing costs and to implement a strong brand image globally. The company was liquidated in 1979.[2] This was the opportunity for Ernest Schneider, an entrepreneur based in Granges and owner of the watch company Sicura SA, to purchase the brand.[3] Using the production capabilities of his company, famous for its imitations of Rolex watches,[4] he started to make Breitling chronographs, refocusing their design and storytelling on the brand's cooperation with aviation. The company enjoyed a successful development. According to Vontobel, it was ranked the twentieth largest Swiss watch brand in 2010, with 260 million francs in sales.[5] After Ernest's death in 2015, his children did not want to pursue the family business. Hence, in 2017, they sold it to an investment fund, which appointed George Kern as the new CEO.[6] Breitling's sales amounted to 418 million francs in 2016 and Kern, a former CEO of IWC, believed he could strengthen this growth by modernizing the brand's communication strategy and keeping it focused on aviation as its core heritage.[7] In 2022, the brand's sales were estimated by Morgan Stanley to be at 860 million francs.

Second, some companies take over declining brands to access new markets or to introduce them to new markets. This is, in particular, the case for non-Swiss companies. Stelux Holdings International is a case in point.[8] This company started manufacturing watch components in Hong Kong during the 1960s. Its desire to upgrade its position and shift from a manufacturer of parts to a fully integrated watchmaker led it to take a 27 per cent stake in Bulova Watch Company in 1976, with the objective of entering the US market. Asia was, however, the easiest market for Stelux. In 1985, it invested in building a dense retail network throughout China and Southeast Asia. Then, it acquired Montres Universal SA in 1988 and relaunched Solvil & Titus in the 1990s, as well as Pronto Watch and Cyma after 2000. These brands, used mostly for non-Swiss-made watches, are still used today by Stelux, but they did not develop successively on the Chinese market.[9] In 2023, Breitling acquired Universal.[10] Unlike Cartier and Breitling, Stelux did not construct a heritage to build on as a development strategy for its new brands. This company simply uses old Swiss brands to sell a large variety of watches, but they do not embody any concept.

The successful takeover and relaunch of declining brands is closely linked to the heritage strategy adopted by the new management. History is, of course, a major source of inspiration to any brand. Most integrate the past, in one way or another, into the construction of their heritage. There are also other dimensions that can be employed to make a successful comeback. Some integrate modern elements into a positioning that remains essentially traditional. The example of Patek Philippe & Cie after its acquisition by family Stern demonstrates that the launch of standardized, mass-produced collections can accompany a discourse on manufacturing tradition and artisanal excellence (see case 4). On the contrary, the example of Chopard after its take-over by the Scheufele family highlights the possibility of launching completely new products (jewellery watches) using an old brand without any reference to the past. It was only later that Chopard was transformed into a brand with a historical heritage (see case 5). Finally, like Hublot, some brands have managed to enter a phase of renewal without talking about their past. The strong concept on which the brand's heritage is built is the foundation of growth (see case 6). So, whatever heritage strategy is adopted, its consistency is an essential factor, as this is what gives strength to the concept implemented. Brands that have failed to find their way back to growth often present a series of inconsistencies or overly profound heritage changes (see case 7).

Case 4: Patek Philippe

Founded in Geneva in 1839, Patek Philippe & Cie today represents the quintessence of the Swiss watchmaking tradition. Its name has spanned almost two centuries, and today it is an undisputed historical leader in the watchmaking industry. However, the firm's current success owes much to the Stern family, who took it over in the early 1930s and radically transformed it to lay the foundations for development in a fast-growing market. The company was on the verge of bankruptcy, and the change of ownership was accompanied by the implementation of a new strategy that gave Patek Philippe & Cie a new lease of life.

The manufacture started through an alliance between a businessman of Polish origin, Antoni Patek (1812–77) and a talented French watchmaker, Jean Adrien Philippe (1815–94).[11] For about half a century, this company experienced growth based on the production of high-precision, complicated pocket watches. It represented the excellence of Swiss watchmaking in international exhibitions and sold its watches to the European aristocracy and American new wealthy classes. A partnership with Tiffany in 1851 contributed to the renown of the brand in the United States, which became the basis of the growth of the brand's manufacture.[12] The 1890s was a decade of transition, with the withdrawal of Philippe from the management of the firm and his death three years later. Although the two founders had disappeared, Patek Philippe & Cie remained a family business belonging to and managed by their heirs. In 1901, the firm was transformed into a joint-stock company under the name Ancienne Manufacture d'Horlogerie Patek, Philippe & Cie SA. Its capital amounted to 1.6 million francs. The first board of directors included Emile Philippe and Antoine Bénassy-Philippe, son and son-in-law of the late Adrien, as well as Antoine Coty, director of production of the company, Jules Perrier, all in Geneva, and Alfred G. Stein, in New York.[13]

The arrival of the second generation at the head of the firm did not lead to any major change. The dependency on the American market continued. In 1895, the company had signed a contract with Alfred G. Stein, a former employee of Tiffany who had founded his own jewellery business. He became the representative of Patek Philippe & Cie in the United States and was appointed to the board when the company was transformed into a joint stock company.[14] He had connections with wealthy American entrepreneurs and was able to distribute watches throughout a dense network of retailers. His orders were transferred to Geneva, where the manufacture answered as much as it could the needs of American customers. This led to the development of a few famous complicated watches, like the models realized for the automobile engineer James Ward Packard and the banker Henry Graves Junior.[15]

However, despite the creation of these specific models for a handful of collectors, the brand started to lose its competitive advantage related to product innovation after the death of Adrien Philippe. Between 1889 and 1905, it received a total of fifteen patents, several of them for parts of complicated movements (perpetual calendar and chronograph).[16] However, after 1905, the company did not carry out breakthrough innovation. It did not get any new patents until the late 1940s. Patek Philippe & Cie basically exploited the knowledge it accumulated during the second part of the nineteenth century. Together with Vacheron & Constantin and a few other small manufacturers, it completely dominated the concours of chronometry organized by the Geneva Observatory, collecting the records and prizes. However, the managers of the firm had a conservative attitude regarding technology and products, best embodied in its late adoption of the wristwatch during the interwar years. They did not consider it as an opportunity to launch new types of luxury watches, unlike emerging competitors such as Rolex, and remained attached to traditional pocket watches. In 1928, while wristwatches amounted to 47 per cent of the export of Swiss watches, their share of Patek Philippe & Cie's production was only 13 per cent.[17] The lack of interest in, or even contempt for, demand transformation would soon prove to be the company's downfall. The crisis that followed the stock market crash of 1929 was to reveal this weakness.

Strongly dependent on the American market, Patek Phillipe & Cie was hit particularly hard by the financial crisis.[18] In 1931, the *Journal de Genève* published a series of articles on the effect of the Great Depression on the local watch industry. In April, it quoted the testimony of one of the directors of Patek Philippe & Cie, who explained that the increase of tariffs in the United States had no real effect on their export because they sold highly expensive watches. However, the financial crisis had terrible effects, as it directly touched the brand's main customers – wealthy Americans – and reduced their orders for luxury watches: Patek Philippe & Cie and similar watch companies 'have been hit quite hard by the financial meltdown, because their customers generally belong to the world of finance and business'.[19] Moreover, in Latin America, the political instability was mentioned as a negative factor for the watch business. Management minimized the effects of the crisis on the employment and explained that watchmakers were producing stocks for better days.[20] However, at the same time, the company faced financial difficulties, probably due to losses in the United States and the lack of liquidities.

This crisis made the business model that had been in place since the late nineteenth century unsustainable. Patek Philippe & Cie was still structured as an artisan workshop.[21] It manufactured a broad range of watches, which made it impossible to rationalize the production of movements and models, unlike what large manufactures like Omega and Longines did at that time.[22] A description of its participation in the Basel Watch Fair in 1933 expresses perfectly this high variety:

> Patek, Philippe et Cie, world-famous for the finish of its mechanisms and the elegant cachet of its cases, presents a selection of the most varied models, from the simplest to the most complicated timepieces. Its superb showcase

contains an assortment of gold and platinum pocket watches, simple and complicated men's and ladies' wristwatches, and jeweled wristwatches. A movement with tourbillon escapement is admired by amateurs of high-precision watchmaking.[23]

The brand was close to bankruptcy in 1931. It needed new investors ready to inject capital into the company. At first, Jacques Le Coultre, a watch manufacturer from Le Sentier, in Vallée de Joux, and supplier of ebauches to Patek Philippe & Cie, invested in the company and joined its board of directors.[24] He was, however, unable to reach an agreement with the Philippe family. Two years later, he left the board.[25] Meanwhile, a new group of investors, led by the brothers Charles Henri and Jean Stern, manufacturers of watch dials in Geneva, had invested in Patek Philippe & Cie. In 1933, having the majority of the shares, they fired Adrien Philippe, minority shareholder and executive director, and engaged a salaried manager with extensive experience in the direction of a modern watch manufacture, Jean Pfister.[26] Charles Stern joined the board and became president in 1935.[27]

The takeover of Patek Philippe & Cie by the Stern family led to a deep transformation within the firm. The brand was reawakened and entered a new era of growth, which continues today. The strategy implemented by the new owners can be characterized by two main pillars: first, the maintenance and strengthening of the core competence of the brand, namely the development, manufacture and sale of complication watches that express the excellence of Swiss watchmaking tradition; second, the transformation of the business model to make it profitable again and increase its competitiveness. Pfister, a former director of Tavannes Watch, one of the largest and most modern watch manufactures in Switzerland at that time, was poached and took charge of the modernization of Patek Philippe & Cie.[28] One of his first actions was the internalization of the conception and production of ebauches. The company had to become independent from its suppliers and to control itself the development of watches. He set up a technical bureau and in 1934 created a first calibre used to equip a new, simple, round-faced wristwatch launched two years before, the Calatrava.[29] This model, the design of which was inspired by Bauhaus, late Art Deco and modernism, embodied the deep transformation of Patek Philippe & Cie. Moreover, although historians lack precise financial data, the Calatrava had undoubtedly been developed for serial production and to provide profits to the firm.

However, the shift towards wristwatches was not limited to the Calatrava. The new management decided on a strategic move towards this product for most of its watches. The company refocused on complicated wristwatches. Numerous new models were launched after 1934.[30] In 1937, the development of a universal watch, realized by the independent watchmaker Louis Cottier, was the symbol of this will to innovate.[31] Moreover, Pfister internally designed new models, like a perpetual calendar wristwatch in 1941 and an automatic movement in 1953.[32] Innovation was back. In

1949, a patent for a balance spring was registered for the first time since 1905. It was followed by twenty-two more patents in the 1950s and eleven in the 1960s.[33]

The position of Patek Philippe & Cie on the luxury market made it possible not to fully rationalize production. On the contrary, keeping a broad variety of complicated wristwatches expressed its identity. However, complicated wristwatches were not handmade separately by artisans. The manufacture introduced a principle of production in very small series based on standardized blueprints and key components. It was able to produce small slots of complicated watches by machine. One of the best examples of this production system is the perpetual calendar chronograph No. 2499. According to Sotheby's, a total of 349 units were produced between 1950 and 1985.[34] While it is a very small number for an industrial product, they were not made by artisans, although they carried the image of the quintessence of the Swiss watchmaking tradition – and enjoy great success in auction sales. This model embodies the application of a few principles of mass production to complicated watches. At the same time, the manufacture continued to participate in the chronometry contests of the Geneva Observatory to maintain its reputation of high precision. Together with complicated watches, it also continued to create jewellery watches for women in cooperation with independent designers, like Gilbert Albert.[35]

Consequently, the new management thus succeeded in creating a complementarity between these complicated watches, which express the brand's excellence, and simpler watches, such as the Calatrava, which benefited from this renown and enabled profits to be made. This balance still exists today and is one of the main sources of the company's success. The auction company Christie's explained in 2014 that 'complicated watch production remained only a small component of Patek Philippe's total production with non-complicated watches representing the great majority of the factory's output'.[36] The relation between the two types of products was thus essential. In 1945, after his visit to the stand of the company at the Basel Watch Fair, the journalist of *Journal de Genève* explained: 'Richly decorated ladies' watches and elegant, well-balanced gentlemen's timepieces bear witness to the successful evolution followed by this House. In this way, it preserves its products with the very sure taste that makes them jewels of the highest class.'[37] Men's watches with simple designs also started to appear in advertisements (see Figure 5.1).

Moreover, the transformation of the business model of the manufacture was not limited to product innovation. Distribution and sales were also considered as a major issue. The company needed to take better control of its relations with its customers. The Stern family, in particular, decided to take direct control over the most important watch market in the world: the United States. In 1937, Henri Stern, son of Charles, was in the United States and took over the import and distribution.[38] Nine years later, in 1946, he founded in New York a specific company dedicated to this business, the Henri Stern Watch Agency.[39]

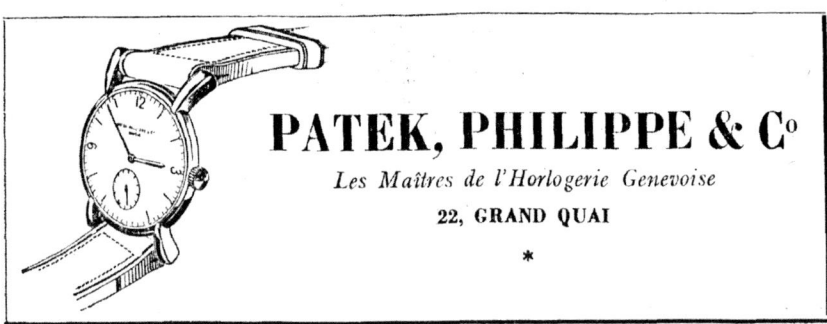

Figure 5.1 Advertisement by Patek Philippe & Cie, 1943.
Source: *Journal de Genève*, 2 December 1943.

The new business model set up between 1935 and 1960 enabled the reawakening of Patek Philippe & Cie. Since this time, its development has continued on three different and complementary products: complicated watches, jewellery watches for women and simple wristwatches. The evolution of the competitive environment – notably, the growing success of newcomers in the luxury watch segment, particularly Rolex and Audemars Piguet – led Patek Philippe & Cie to innovate. It continued to invest in keeping its image as the representative of watchmaking excellence – for example, with the development of the most complicated watch in the world (1989), a special auction organized by Antiquorum to communicate this tradition to a worldwide audience (1989) and, more recently, the opening of the Patek Philippe Museum (2001). At the same time, the manufacture launched new generations of iconic goods in order to strengthen its visibility on the global luxury market and to increase its profitability. The jewellery watch Ellipse d'Or (1968) and the luxury sports watch Nautilus (1976) are probably the most successful examples of this renewal.

Case 5: Making Chopard a jewellery brand

We discussed the difficulty of launching new brands in the field of jewellery watches in the previous chapter (see case 2). Since the end of the Second World War, only two companies have been able to achieve such success: one was a watchmaker specialized in the manufacturing of complicated movements that diversified to jewellery (Piaget), and the other was a German jeweller who took over a small watch company based in Geneva, Chopard, and relaunched it as a jewellery watch brand.

The roots of this watch company go back to a watch assembly workshop founded in 1860 in Sonvilier, in the Vallon of Saint-Imier, by Louis-Ulysse Chopard, aged twenty-four years old.[40] His company was officially registered in 1883 under the name L.U. Chopard.[41] He was an ambitious watchmaker, protecting his brand in 1884 and taking part in the International Exhibition of Anvers in 1885.[42] After 1900, he developed various models of watches, movements and hands, which showed his will to innovate through specific designs.[43] He also obtained two patents, in 1914 and 1915, for mechanisms of watches.[44] After his death in 1915, the company was pursued by his son, Louis-Paul, who in 1921 opened a subsidiary in La Chaux-de-Fonds, where the headquarters were transferred the following year.[45] The objective was probably to be closer to suppliers of watch components and subcontractors, who clustered in this city. Paul-André Chopard, grandson of the founder, took over the family firm in 1936.[46] In 1937, the company was transferred to Geneva, following the example of numerous small watch assembly makers who wanted to be closer to their customers, Geneva having established itself as a centre where watch wholesalers from all the world came to discuss business with their suppliers.[47]

Small in size, Chopard struggled to remain competitive after the Second World War, against a backdrop of the growth of global brands on the world markets (cf. Chapter 3). The virtual absence of Chopard from *Europa Star*'s archives before the early 1960s is a perfect illustration of its difficulties and weaknesses. It is mentioned only once – in a table of jubilee brands published in 1950 – but its activities and products did not attract the attention of the watch magazine at the time.[48] The company was very small: it had only five employees in 1963.[49] As Paul-André's children had no interest in continuing the management of the family business, he decided in 1963 to sell it to a German jeweller, Karl Scheufele, who wanted to acquire a watch factory based in Switzerland. A new joint stock company, Le petit-fils de L.U. Chopard & Cie SA, with a capital of 50,000 francs, was founded in 1964.[50]

Karl Scheufele was himself the third-generation owner of a family firm from Pforzheim, in Germany, founded in 1904. Like many enterprises in this city, his company specialized in the manufacture of jewellery and watchbands.[51] Until then, he had subcontracted the manufacture of movements, as had other jewellers at that time, such as Cartier and Tiffany. By acquiring a small Swiss watch manufacturer at a good price, Scheufele sought to internalize watchmaking know-how and take full control of the market launch of jewellery-watch collections.

In the mid-1960s, Chopard was relaunched as a jewellery brand, a few years after Piaget had opened a boutique on Rue du Rhône in Geneva (1959). It took part in various fairs around the world, showing its various models of watches, especially for ladies. At the same time, however, Scheufele continued to use his own name for his jewellery collections. The German company, Karl Scheufele GmbH, continued the production of jewellery. The knowledge acquired for the development and production of branded jewellery led the Scheufele family to create a new business in 1970 with a renowned German gold jeweller from Pforzheim, Geor Lauer, with whom the company Laudier SA was founded in Geneva.[52] This shows the ambition of Scheufele to develop a competitive advantage in the branded jewellery segment, in which watches had to play an important role.

The mid-1970s marked the first turning point in the company's history. While the Swiss watch industry sank into crisis, Chopard opened a new factory in Meyrin in 1975. The company employed 170 people – against five when it took over Chopard in 1963. It had built a competitive business model, based on the development of small series of jewellery watches – about thirty pieces per model – for a total yearly production of about 15,000 watches and gross sales of 35 million francs.[53] The division of work between German workshops (golden bracelets and jewellery dials) and the factory in Geneva (watchcase manufacturing and watch assembly) enabled the Scheufele family to have full control of product development and production.

Moreover, the mid-1970s were also marked by the launch of a new jewellery watch that would become an iconic product and lead Chopard to a period of fast growth in the next decade: the Happy Diamonds. This model, equipped with diamonds moving freely between the dial and the glass of the watch, was launched in 1976. At the beginning, this watch was not specifically designed for ladies. Some models for men were also marketed.[54] However, the Happy Diamonds soon became very successful as a ladies' jewellery watch (Figure 5.2). It contributed to establishing Chopard as a brand for ladies in the minds of the general public, despite the company also launching elegant sporty watches for men, like the collections St. Moritz (1980) and Gstaad (1986).[55]

A new milestone was reached with the arrival of Karl-Friedrich and Caroline Scheufele at the head of the company in the early 1990s. It was reorganized with the foundation of Chopard Holding SA to supervise and manage the different assets of the family.[56] Following on from the Happy Diamonds collection, they developed Chopard in two complementary directions: as a watch brand that expressed the tradition of Swiss watchmaking excellence, under the direction of Karl-Friedrich, and as a jewellery brand, under Caroline.

One of the goals of the diversification towards the development of traditional mechanical watches was to increase the share of watches for men in Chopard

Figure 5.2 Advertisement for Chopard, 1988.

Source: *Europa Star Asia*, no. 171, 1988 © Archives Europa Star.

Note: The Happy Diamonds model experienced great success and contributed to the establishment of Chopard as a brand of jewellery watches. However, at the same time, it made it a brand focused on ladies' watches.

sales, while the success of Happy Diamonds had clearly made it a ladies' watch brand for the public. In 1997, men's watches amounted to about 20 per cent of the value and 35 per cent of the volume of sales.[57] The management of the company decided in 1993 to acquire the knowledge necessary for the in-house development of mechanical watches. Karl-Friedrich Scheufele explained that 'we had to reinforce our watchmaking essence in relation to our image as a jeweller, and we had to make our own movements, because it's our philosophy to make everything – or almost everything – in-house'.[58] Until then, Chopard produced either quartz watches or mechanical watches using components supplied by Swatch Group. Hence, Chopard cooperated with the artisan watchmaker Michel Parmigiani to create a prototype of an automatic movement for a men's watch, which was named L.U.C. as a tribute to the founder of the company. Three years later, in 1996, a new company, Chopard Manufacture SA, was founded in Fleurier, Val de Travers (canton of Neuchâtel), for the production of this movement.[59] The first watch equipped with this movement was launched in 1997. Since then, it has been used for the best-quality mechanical watches for men developed by Chopard. Moreover, in 2008, a second manufacturing company, Fleurier Ebauches SA, was founded in Fleurier for the production of basic mechanical movements.[60] As Swatch Group had announced in 2002 its will to stop delivering components of movements, it became necessary to invest in securing the manufacture of movements.[61] These two firms enabled Chopard to control the production of mechanical watches. Since then, it has successively launched various models, particularly for men, that build on these capabilities. New versions of L.U.C. complicated watches, Mille Miglia sports watches (launched first in 1988 through a partnership with the Italian vintage car race) and Alpine Eagle luxury sports watches (launched in 2019) are regularly advertised. The ambitions of the Scheufele family in the development of luxury mechanical watches led to the launch of a new heritage brand (Ferdinand Berthoud), similar to the cases discussed in Chapter 6. The name of this famous manufacturer of marine chronometers in the second part of the eighteenth century has been used for the creation of special mechanical pieces, certified as chronometers by COSC. However, although the company Chronomètres Ferdinand Berthoud SA was founded in 2009 within Chopard Manufacture SA, the brand and its products are clearly separated from Chopard.[62]

Besides the development of mechanical watches, Chopard continued and strengthened its position as a jeweller through various actions. In 1997, for example, it presented the world's most expensive watch at the Basel Fair, the Fleur model, valued at around $25 million. But it was, above all, its partnership with the Cannes Film Festival, for which Chopard has been producing the Palme d'Or in Geneva since 1998, that stood out (see Figure 5.3). The previous year, Caroline Scheufele had proposed redesigning the trophy given to the winner.[63] This renewed the visual identity of the festival and contributed to establishing Chopard as a jewellery brand. Moreover, fifteen years later, Chopard was a first mover in the use of ethical gold and

Figure 5.3 Jewellers at the Cannes Festival, 1998.

Source: *International Jeweller*, no. 229, 1998 © Archives Europa Star.

Note: The partnership with the Cannes Festival was a major step for the recognition of Chopard as a jewellery brand.

other materials from fair trade – such a position fitting particularly well with the dominant ideology of show business. In 2013, the company launched a Green Carpet collection at Cannes with jewels made from Fairmined gold (a label certified since 2004) and precious stones whose suppliers were accredited by the Responsible Jewellery Council (an organization formed in 2005 by fourteen companies, including Cartier, De Beers and Tiffany). In 2018, Chopard decided to use only ethical gold for its jewellery.[64] The brand's aims embody sustainability, including for watches – it announced in April 2023 its objective to source mostly ethical steel for its watches.[65] Chopard's jewels are produced in the production centres of the company, which are based in Geneva and in Pforzheim.

The twofold strategy adopted by Karl-Friedrich and Caroline in the early 1990s has been successful. They were able to establish Chopard as both a watch brand and jewellery brand on the global market. According to the consulting company Euromonitor, Chopard was the world's sixth-largest luxury jewellery company in 2013–22.[66] As for watches, while gross sales amounted to about 45 million francs in 1979, they were estimated to be 409 million in 2006.[67] According to Morgan Stanley, for the years 2017–22, Chopard was nearly always ranked within the top twenty largest Swiss watch brands (except in 2019). In 2022, 410 million in gross sales made it the twentieth largest brand, behind Van Cleef & Arpels (521 million) but before Bulgari (371 million) and Piaget (265 million). Its double position as a jewellery watch and a traditional mechanical watch manufacturer is undoubtedly a major reason for its success against rival brands – Van Cleef & Arpels having a special position as a producer of highly expensive watches (with an average retail price 2.7 times higher than Piaget, 4.1 times higher than Chopard and 5.6 times higher than Bulgari).[68]

Case 6: Revival based on a concept: Hublot

A number of new luxury watch brands, especially for niche products, are not based on the exploitation of the past within a heritage strategy. From Richard Mille to Parmigiani to Andersen Genève, many brands were developed outside of the widespread narrative about the embodiment of the Swiss historical craft tradition. Rather, they were built on a clear and strong concept. Hublot is an excellent illustration of how new management may reawaken a brand by focusing on its core concept, without using history as the heart of its narrative. Here also, the key person in this revival process was Jean-Claude Biver. At the end of 2003, after more than a decade in Swatch Group, in the context of the arrival of Hayek's third generation in the business – Marc A. Hayek had been appointed marketing manager (2001) and CEO (2002) of Blancpain[69] – Biver resigned from Swatch and looked for new challenges. In January 2004, he announced his plan to help Franck Muller recover growth.[70] This was, however, only a short-term project and, in June 2004, Biver announced that he had invested in a small company owning the brand Hublot and would take an executive position to reawaken this brand.[71]

Hublot was a watch brand launched in 1980 by Carlo Crocco, an Italian designer who had worked for the Binda Group before moving to Switzerland.[72] In 1980, he took over a financial company established in Lugano, Nemi SA, for which he had been a board member since 1978, and registered the brand and the logo for Hublot.[73] The following year, in 1981, he moved his business to Geneva, becoming president of MDM SA, a small firm founded the previous year with a capital of 50,000 francs, to which the brand Hublot was transmitted.[74] The 1970s had seen the arrival of several types of luxury sports watches, using mostly steel – the Royal Oak being the most well known today. Crocco had the idea of engaging in this business, but with a new kind of product: a watch equipped with a yellow gold case and a black rubber strap. This Hublot watch was presented at the Basel Fair in 1980.[75] MDM explained the characteristics of its new watch in an advertisement published at this occasion (see Figure 5.4):

> Here is a marine watch with captivating lines, which will charm those with the most demanding tastes. The marriage of gold, steel, and rubber produces a provocative style which has character. Its dial in the shape of a port-hole will add a dash of the sea to all 'thoroughbred' sportsmen. Its strap, fitted with a special and luxurious catch, its quartz movement and its water-tightness to a pressure of 10 atmospheres guarantees total security for sporting use.[76]

In order to organize the growth of his business, in 1982, Crocco established a second firm in Geneva, at the same address, Montres MDM SA, with a capital of 200,000 francs, which increased to two million francs in 1983.[77] This company was in charge of production, while MDM SA focused on the management of patents and brands, as

A HUBLOT: a watch with character

Here is a marine watch with captivating lines, which will charm those with the most demanding tastes. The marriage of gold, steel, and rubber produces a provocative style which has character.

Its dial in the shape of a port-hole will add a dash of the sea to all "thoroughbred" sportsmen. Its strap, fitted with a special and luxurious catch, its quartz movement and its water-tightness to a pressure of 10 atmospheres guarantees total security for sporting use.

HUBLOT
MDV — Geneva

Hublot watch seen from all angles.

 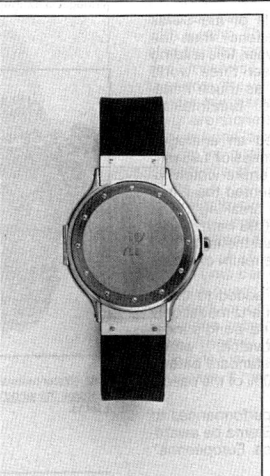 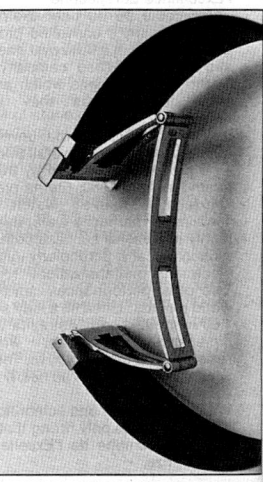

Figure 5.4 Advertisement for Hublot, 1980.

Source: *The Eastern Jeweler and Watchmaker*, no. 177, 1980 © Archives Europa Star.

Note: The Hublot brand was born of a specific design, which the company communicated intensively in its early years. However, these stylistic elements were not part of a broader concept.

well as marketing and sales. This twofold organization, adopted probably for financial and fiscal reasons, was not uncommon in the Swiss watch industry at that time – Rolex was its best embodiment.[78] In 1985, production facilities were moved outside of Geneva, into the neighbouring town of Nyon. Crocco founded MDM Fabrication SA, with one million francs.[79] In 1989, it increased its capital to three million francs and merged with MDM Montres SA.[80]

In the 1980s, MDM focused on the development of watches based on the unique style of Hublot, launching various versions of this product. For example, a chronograph was marketed in 1988. It followed a classical luxury strategy, signing contracts with celebrities to wear its models, like King of Spain Juan Carlos, Hollywood star Eddy Murphy and German soccer player Karl-Heinz Rumenigge.[81] The idea of combining 'traditional Swiss workmanship with high technology and styling' was kept over the years, with the company stressing that its watches were characterized by an 'impressive beauty and a virtual indestructibility'.[82]

However, during his first decade of activity in Switzerland, Crocco did not focus on a single brand. The sales of Hublot watches were probably not high enough to ensure the profitability of his business. Hence, in 1988, MDM launched a second collection, Thorr watches, named after the Nordic god of thunder, for products full of technological innovations (watch crystal filtering the sun's ultraviolet rays, new waterproof system, laser-shaped and Kevlar-reinforced 'unbreakable' strap, etc.).[83] The next year, Crocco also worked for another company related to the Italian market, Montres Breil SA, founded in Zurich in 1982, which developed a Boxer Chronograph in 1989.[84] This brand had been launched in Italy in 1968 and used for luxury fashion watches, then introduced into Switzerland, the United States and Japan in the early 1980s. The idea was to use Italian design and Swiss watch technology. Crocco was designer and manager of the firm.[85]

These additional activities did not allow MDM to find a path to growth, and Crocco refocused on Hublot in the 1990s by multiplying the variations of its iconic model. In 1993, he developed a model made in platinum and presented a collection of jewellery watches for ladies.[86] The variety continued to increase in the following years, with, for example, Hublot Erotique (1994), Hublot GMT (1994), Hublot Email with automatic movement and Côte de Genève decoration (1995), Hublot Aluminium (1995), Hublot Chronograph with steel bracelet (1996), Hublot Grand Quantième (2000) and Hublot Art Collection, in cooperation with talented artisans (2003).[87] The multiplication of models and designs made the identity of the brand more and more vague.

Moreover, the communication strategy of MDM was unrelated to Hublot's brand management. It was driven by Crocco's highly responsible values.[88] He did not want his enterprise to be a mere money-making activity. Its contribution to society was an important goal of the entrepreneur. In 1989, Crocco launched a Thorr Prize to celebrate personalities that supported the cause of freedom and democracy around the world. Mikhail Gorbachev (1989), Juan Carlos of Spain (1990), Judge Antonio Di

Pietro (1992), Sinn Fein President Gerry Adams (1993) and Algerian journalist Salima Ghezali (1998), among others, have received the award.[89] Ten years later, in 1999, Crocco created the MDM Foundation, with a capital of one million Swiss francs, to help children in the Third World and to award a Hublot Prize to a personality or an organization that supported children in need.[90] Although highly commendable in their aim to improve our world, Crocco's humanitarian actions developed outside of any purpose related to brand management.

At the beginning of the twenty-first century, MDM was unable to find the right strategy to enter a phase of growth, while the market for luxury watches was booming. Hublot's sales were stagnating. Their volume amounted to about 12,000 watches in 1996 and 15,000 watches in 2004. Moreover, it did not generate profits.[91] Something needed to be done to rescue the brand and the firm. Cocco's encounter with Jean-Claude Biver, the former boss of Blancpain and the man who relaunched Omega in the 1990s, was the opportunity to revive Hublot. In 2004, Biver invested in the company and took over the reins.[92] He accepted an executive position in MDM SA and was appointed member of the board of MDM Fabrication SA. The same year, he renamed both firms Hublot SA.[93] Today, there are still two Hublot SA companies, one in Geneva managing intellectual property, sales and marketing, and one in Nyon manufacturing watches.[94]

Biver had an interest in Hublot because Crocco had succeeded in launching and keeping intact an iconic product: the brand was based on a single product (a luxury watch with a rubber strap), with a strong visual identity (a case in the shape of a porthole), available in various models. He saw the potential to develop Hublot into something new, explaining in 2004 that it was 'a mono-product brand, but transformable, adaptable and the original concept has not taken on a single wrinkle since its creation'.[95] According to Biver, the first important point was to clearly define the concept of the brand, what made its heritage and its identity. Based on the idea of a luxury watch using gold and rubber, he developed the concept of 'fusion'. Hublot thus became the embodiment of fusion in a large perspective, as argued by Biver:

> From now on, this Fusion is our directive, and must be interpreted in all domains: in materials – it doesn't matter which ones, as long as there is a fusion of two elements – and in movements, where the same principle applies, offering a fusion of tradition and savoir-faire inherited from the past with the future, the infinite. Think for a minute what this means. We will never make only traditional, and we will never make only futuristic. We will fuse them both together. Our ambition is to become the reference for fusion in watchmaking. It is our religion. We want to develop this concept of fusion. We want to promote fusion and demonstrate the richness that it conveys. I want to become the Pope of Fusion.[96]

At the Baselworld Watch Fair 2005, Hublot presented a collection of rejuvenated models of its watches, based on the traditional design developed by Crocco. At the same time, Biver announced the launch of a new model that would express the new departure of the brand: the Big Bang. This oversized watch, which combines various kinds of materials and rubber, was presented to a few selected journalists and launched a few weeks later.[97] At the end of year, it won the prize for the best design at the Grand Prix d'Horlogerie de Genève. It became an immediate commercial success.

The 'Art of Fusion', as Biver called it, led Hublot to develop various new materials, in-house and in cooperation with the Swiss Federal Institute of Technology of Lausanne (EPFL). In particular, Hublot designed high-tech ceramics in various colours, scratch-resistant 18-carat gold and synthetic sapphires.[98] These technological innovations enabled the brand to offer innovative products in the exclusive luxury segment – products that met with phenomenal success (see Figure 5.5).

Sponsorship was reorganized as another expression of fusion – very far from the humanitarian goals adopted originally by Crocco – particularly during the first year following the arrival of Biver. In 2004, the first contract with a sports player was in yachting, with Biver arguing that this sport was the fusion between two elements (wind and water).[99] Two years later, Hublot became the first luxury watch brand to be an official sponsor of soccer events, clubs and players. This sport had often been seen as too popular for classical luxury brands, which preferred to make partnerships with sports that had an elite image, such as tennis and polo. However, after 2000, soccer experienced a deep transformation and became a universal sport that transcended social classes and nations. From this perspective, it could be seen as another incarnation of fusion. Moreover, soccer players have become celebrities. Kylian Mbappé is not only one of the world's best soccer players but also an ambassador and fashion model. For Hublot, the sponsorship of major events and famous footballers also contributed significantly to the brand's reputation. However, over the last decade, the concept of fusion has not been as clear as it used to be as a driver of sponsorship. Hublot, having been established as a renowned luxury watch brand, started to extend its partnership to a broad range of sportsmen and artists, based on a more general idea of the quest for excellence and performance.[100]

Hublot's brand revival based on the clear definition of a core idea as a concept has been very successful. The turnover of the brand rose from around 29 million francs in 2004 to 150 million in 2007, leading LVMH to buy the company in 2008.[101] Biver withdrew in 2011. He was replaced by Ricardo Guadalupe, who had been appointed chief operating officer of Hublot in 2004 and worked with him to relaunch the brand. Hublot continued to grow, reaching sales estimated at 744 million francs in 2022, making it the twelfth-largest watch brand in the world in terms of turnover.[102] As for the volume, it was estimated to be 54,000 watches in 2022 – nearly four times more than when Biver took over the company.

Figure 5.5 Advertisement for Hublot, 2005.

Source: *Europa Star Europe*, no. 274, 2005 © Archives Europa Star.

Note: Following the arrival of Jean-Claude Biver at the head of Hublot, the brand's stylistic identity became the visual and material expression of the concept of fusion. The brand was relaunched with a subtle blend of continuity and transformation.

Case 7: Failed attempts to relaunch sleeping beauties: Corum and Ebel

Besides the success stories presented above, there are numerous attempts to reawaken brands after a takeover that failed. This emphasizes that the mere fact of buying a declining brand that owns a bright history is not sufficient to encounter success. In order to analyse in detail the conditions of failure, we discuss here two brands currently owned by Chinese and American companies, respectively: Corum and Ebel.

Corum apparently had all the ingredients for a successful relaunch: an original history and position in the watch industry, based on a genius designer (René Bannwart) and iconic products (Golden Bridge and Admiral's Cup). Indeed, while Gerald Genta is acclaimed worldwide as the world's first watch designer, Corum would have the potential to challenge this narrative and establish itself as a disruptive design innovator. Born in Zurich in 1915 and having worked for Patek Philippe & Cie since 1933, René Bannwart was engaged by Omega in 1940 as the head of its Service de Créations, the first specific department dedicated to the design of watch collections in a major manufacture.[103] He oversaw the launch of several collections, including the Seamaster and Constellation. In 1955, Bannwart left Omega to take over the management of a watch company opened in 1924 in La Chaux-de-Fonds by his family.[104] The company was renamed Ries, Bannwart & Co.[105] Using the brand name Corum, the company launched innovative watch designs, such as the Coin Watch (1960), the Golden Bridge (1979) and the Admiral's Cup (1983). Corum had been able to establish itself on the niche market of luxury fashion watches. The Golden Bridge, presented as 'pure and wholly horological beauty', was developed through the cooperation of various independent actors, like artisan watchmaker Vincent Calabrese and Seitz SA (see Figure 5.6).[106] As for the Admiral's Cup watch, it enabled Corum to develop a partnership with yachting and to strengthen the luxury image of the brand. This position made it possible for Corum not to be severely touched by the crisis that threatened the existence of the Swiss watch industry in the early 1980s. In 1990, Jean-René Bannwart, son of René and owner of the firm at that time, explained that 'design and creation have always been our company's strength. Year after year, we make a point of offering original items that meet the spirit of the times and customer tastes but never knowingly encroach upon the findings and inspirations of other upmarket companies.'[107] The family firm experienced an impressive development, growing from five employees in 1955 to ninety in 1992.

In the 1990s, Corum pursued its development on the basis of the exploitation of its iconic models, like the Golden Bridge and the Admiral's Cup, and the development of new products. However, since the early 1980s, the company had based its success mostly on Japanese and Asian markets: their share amounted to some 40 per cent of sales in 1998.[108] The decline of luxury sales in Japan due to the financial crisis and economic stagnation had a deep impact on Corum. The company had multiplied

Figure 5.6 Advertisement for Corum, 1980.

Source: *Europa Star Europe*, no. 124, 1980 © Archives Europa Star.

Note: The Golden Bridge model became an iconic product of Corum. Together with the Admiral's Cup, it was used for several decades as the expression of the innovativeness of the brand in matters of design.

models, and its production was not rationalized like large firms. In 1999, *Europa Star* explained the weakness of such a business model:

> With the exception of the Admiral's Cup line, a good revenue generator, Corum's products are composed of a multitude of very specific models, produced in small or even tiny limited series which are consequently difficult to manage. On the other hand, this 'weakness' is also seen as one of the brand's strengths. Corum has always assumed the risk of having a collection too diversified and exclusive rather than confining itself to an easily changeable two-product line. Unfortunately, the brand is now paying the price of its exclusivity.[109]

Hence, Corum had no choice but to drastically reduce its workforce in 1998. In 1999, it refocused the brand on a few core models and gave up the broad range of creations it used to manufacture. The Admiral's Cup was chosen in 1999 as the iconic model of the brand.[110] However, it was not enough. The company needed fresh capital, and it came from a businessman based in California: Severin Wunderman.

Born in Belgium, Wunderman started his business in the United States making golden jewellery during the 1950s and diversifying to private-label watches in the 1960s. This activity led him to sign a licence agreement with Gucci for the manufacture and sale of watches for this Italian fashion brand. This business was very successful, and Gucci acquired it in 1997.[111] Wunderman was thus looking for a new opportunity in the late 1990s. Corum's need for capital was the perfect occasion. In 2000, Wunderman became president of the board and executive manager of Montres Corum SA.[112] The most important change introduced under his management was the launch of a new model for the mid-segment market. Wunderman transformed distribution, working more closely with retailers, but kept the brand focused on design and jewellery watches. He also relaunched the Admiral's Cup and made this iconic watch available in various models.[113] Corum experienced a new phase of success and moved upmarket, developing a few limited series of complicated watches in cooperation with independent artisan watchmakers. Between 1999 and 2010, sales grew from a maximum of 35 million francs to some 130 million.[114]

The death of Severin Wunderman in 2008 should not have been a major break. He had organized the transition – his son Michael had entered the company in 2001 and he had appointed Antonio Calce as a CEO in 2007.[115] However, the Wunderman family had no interest in pursuing its engagement with the watch industry, especially as the brand had not been profitable since 2009.[116] In 2013, they sold Corum to the Chinese company China Haidian, later renamed Citychamp Watch & Jewelry Group. This firm, headquartered in Hong Kong, is one of the most important watch distributors in China, with watch sales growing from 123 million HK$ in 2005 to a peak at 2.7 billion HK$ in 2016. It then entered a phase of decline (2.2 billion in 2019 and 1.2 billion in 2022).[117] Corum was purchased in the context of a fast expansion. The strategy of the Chinese group was not only to build an ever-expanding retail network in China but also to take over firms in order to own a diversified portfolio. It already controlled two major Chinese brands (Rossini and Ebohr) and successively acquired the Swiss companies Eterna (2011), Corum (2013) and Rotary (2014).[118]

The change of ownership of Corum occurred in a difficult financial context, and Citychamps' sales started to decline three years after the acquisition. The will to develop new mechanical complicated movements and to promote the brand in China and Southeast Asia required massive investment. Corum was therefore a loss-making brand in 2013–15.[119] Consequently, the Chinese owner dismissed Antonio Calce, but it was unable to keep a new executive manager for more than a few years. The lack of clear management direction, as well as the lack of knowledge and experience of the group in luxury brand management (the attempt to create its own Swiss-made brand, Codex, in 2010 had been a disaster) had a negative impact on Corum. Over the last decade, the new owner has been incapable of building the consistent heritage on which Corum should have been developed. Consequently, the sales of the brand dropped from 130 million francs in 2010 to 50 million in 2017. Since 2018, Corum has disappeared from Morgan Stanley's ranking of the top-largest Swiss watch brands.[120]

Another example of a Swiss renowned watch brand in the second part of the twentieth century that lost its lustre after a takeover is Ebel. The roots of this brand go back to a small family firm founded in La Chaux-de-Fonds in 1911 by Eugène Blum and his wife Alice Lévy, under the name Fabrique Ebel Blum & Cie.[121] Until the end of the 1960s, it grew, developing a broad range of watches, as most small family firms used to do at that time.

The 1970s was the first major turning point in the history of Ebel. Pierre-Alain Blum, grandson of the founders, was appointed CEO of the family firm.[122] While the Swiss watch industry started to face competition from Japan and the advent of quartz watches, he decided to drastically transform his company and to make Ebel an accessible luxury brand. This was made possible by a cooperation agreement signed with Cartier in 1977, according to which Ebel would supply the French jeweller with quartz watches.[123] Cartier had been taken over a few years before by a group of French businessmen who had adopted a new growth strategy based on building a global luxury brand embodied by accessories. The demand for watches was booming.[124]

For Blum, this partnership was the perfect opportunity to develop his company. He invested in the expansion of production capacity, engaging in the mass production of quartz watches, which could be also used for his own brand. Between 1970 and 1981, his workforce grew from eighty to 450 employees.[125] Blum reinvested the profit from his business with Cartier in repositioning Ebel as an accessible luxury brand. In the 1980s, the core of his price segment was 1000–1500 francs.[126] Ebel started to sponsor tennis and golf events, and he was one of the first to develop partnerships with sports players (German tennis player Boris Becker), celebrities from culture (opera singer Barbara Hendricks) and movie stars (US actress Sharon Stone) as ambassadors. In 1978, Blum developed the concept of the 'Architects of Time', emphasizing that his watches were developed as pieces of art that answered the basic principles of modern architecture in terms of construction, proportions and lines (see Figure 5.7).[127] To strengthen this concept, in 1986 Blum purchased the Turkish Villa in La Chaux-de-Fonds, a house made by Le Corbusier (himself born in this city), for holding public relations events. This villa and the brand Ebel were presented as sharing similar values: a manifesto for pure art, stripped of passing fashions, focused on essential functions.

Buoyed by this success, Pierre-Alain Blum started to diversify into new businesses. He invested in sports equipment, real estate in Europe and the United States, movie production and banking. All these participations were controlled by a holding company founded in 1987, Sogespa SA, and a financial firm organized the following year, Ebel Finance SA.[128] These investments were, however, loss-making, and Blum had no choice but to sell his shares. In 1994, Investcorp, a private equity firm from Bahrain that had taken over several luxury companies in financial difficulties (Chaumet, Gucci, Tiffany, etc.), acquired Ebel.[129] Its brand value was excellent: it employed some 900 people in 1994, and its sales amounted to about 250 million francs in 1996.[130] However, a change of management at the head of the firm led to a change of strategy. Blum left Ebel in 1996.[131] The 'Architects of Time' was abandoned for a new communication concept based on the idea of time and travel, as explained by the new team in charge of Ebel:

> one is witnessing the end of a superficial period, turned entirely towards outside images and superficiality. The consumer's relationship to the product is intensified and personalized; discretion becomes a quality; imagination comes back into the foreground. The growing share of personal budgets for travelling, escape and culture indicate the 'time, a new luxury product, has been born'.[132]

Travel was made the new concept of Ebel, with the objective to position Ebel in a poetic and elitist setting. In 1999, Investcorp sold Ebel to LVMH, which decided to make a strategic move to watches.[133] The new management changed again the collections in 2001 and the advertising campaign in 2003.[134] The objective was then to make Ebel a ladies' watch, while TAG Heuer, also purchased by LVMH in 1999, would make men's watches.[135] This was again a deep change, as men's watches represented about half of Ebel's sales until that time. However, this new position was not successful and, in 2004, LVMH disposed Ebel to the American company Movado Group.

Movado specialized in the production and sales of fashion watches under licence, like Coach, Hugo Boss and Tommy Hilfiger. It relied essentially on the US market (more than 50 per cent of gross sales in 2005).[136] Its objective, with the acquisition of Ebel, was to enter the luxury market. The brand re-launched men's watches in 2006.[137] Finally, in 2010, Ebel decided to return to the concept of 'The Architects of

Figure 5.7 Advertisement for Ebel.

Source: *Europa Star China*, no. 33, 1994 © Archives Europa Star.

Note: The Architects of Time was a concept that made Ebel one of the most successful watch brands in the accessible luxury segment in the early 1990s. It connected quality watchmaking and the elegance of simple lines.

Time' and to focus communication on the design of its watches, their materials and the beauty of their lines.[138]

All these dramatic changes of identity and positioning over the last three decades had a disastrous effect on the brand's competitiveness. According to Vontobel Equity Research, Ebel's sales had dropped to 130 million in 1999 and 90 million in 2004. In 2019, it did not appear in Morgan Stanley's ranking of the top fifty largest Swiss watch brands – the lowest rank of which had 40 million sales.

Conclusion

The various examples of companies in decline being revived through a new branding strategy by new owners perfectly illustrate the importance of a clear vision and the construction of a coherent heritage. Some company directors have developed new iconic products that give the brand visibility with a fairly wide audience, thereby ensuring improved profitability. Examples include Patek Philippe & Cie's Calatrava and Chopard's Happy Diamonds. In other cases, it was the repositioning or modernization of old iconic models that ensured a phase of growth. Biver transformed Hublot into the expression of the fusion concept, while Wunderman gave a second life to Corum's Admiral's Cup. As for the Stern family, they revived the tradition of grand complications horology in the form of wristwatches.

By contrast, the difficulties, and even the inability, of certain management teams to relaunch brands is often the result of the absence of a clear heritage strategy (Corum after its takeover by China Haidian) or the multiplication of repositioning (Ebel after its takeover by Investcorp). Historical continuity is not a priori a necessary condition. Chopard enjoyed a major boom with jewellery watches long before it began developing a collection of men's watches inspired by the family tradition with its in-house L.U.C. movement. The revival of declining companies through the adoption of new brand strategies by new owners therefore depends more on the coherence of the heritage than on absolute continuity with tradition.

Chapter 6

Creating new brands from heritage

The third main way of waking up a sleeping beauty is not by relaunching a brand as such but by exploiting the name of a famous creator who has disappeared. For the most part, these are eighteenth- and nineteenth-century watchmakers who left their mark on the history of watchmaking through their inventions and products. As most of them were active before the advent of a system of legal protection for trademarks, their name was often not perpetuated after their death, even if in some cases companies continued their activities for a time.

Business models based on the exploitation of heritage brands are therefore special in that they offer considerable scope for manoeuvre. There are many different ways of paying tribute to deceased watchmakers. The case of Breguet is, of course, the most emblematic (see case 8). Abraham-Louis Breguet is one of the most famous figures in watchmaking history. In the 1970s, the name was used to launch a brand in tribute to him that already had the main features of heritage brands: a focus on exclusive luxury, the creation of watch models inspired by the master's creations and a discourse on classical culture. The British master watchmakers (see case 9) and semi-legendary figures such as Daniel JeanRichard (see case 10) are another source of inspiration. These examples also highlight the development of heritage brands whose links with the figures they seek to honour are vague, to say the least, which is not without its management problems. Finally, some heritage brands are built on a technical basis (see case 11). This generally makes it possible to develop a coherent narrative that integrates the excellence of the watchmaker one is seeking to honour and the products launched from this perspective.

Case 8: Breguet

Although Abraham-Louis Breguet (1747–1823) is widely celebrated today as one of the greatest watchmakers in modern history, his name was known only to a handful of museum curators and artisan watchmakers in the early 1970s. Beyond these insider circles, his fame had disappeared for many decades. The name belonged to the history of the watch, not to a special company, like other famous artisans from this industry. Hence, in 1953, Rolex used Breguet and his Marie-Antoinette watch in an advertisement to argue that the Rolex Oyster was somehow the heir of Breguet's watchmaking tradition (cf. Figure 6.1). In an industry that favoured technological innovation and the most modern designs, what was the value of the name of a watchmaker active at the crossroads of the eighteenth and nineteenth centuries?

When the Parisian jewellery house Chaumet took over Maison Breguet in 1970, the name was essentially associated with aviation among the French general public. After the death of Abraham-Louis in 1823, the watch company was carried on by his son, Louis Antoine, and his grandson, Louis Clément François. However, the company had lost its sense of innovation. Unlike Patek Philippe & Cie, which established itself in the mid-nineteenth century as the new brand embodying the genius of mechanical watchmaking, Breguet went through a phase of stagnation and decline. Louis Clément François, who took over the management of the company in 1833, was more interested in electrical devices and physics than in watchmaking itself. So, in 1870, he sold the watchmaking workshop to his production manager, an English watchmaker named Edward Brown.[1] The Breguet dynasty continued its work in the field of industrial appliances and equipment, with Louis Charles founding the Breguet Aviation company in 1911. This company flourished and merged with Dassault in 1971.[2] Much more than watchmaking, aeronautics made Breguet a major name in French industry in the twentieth century.

As for the former watchmaking workshop, it was renamed Brown & Cie in 1870. It was a small company with a capital of 120,000 francs, belonging to Edward Brown and an unknown investor.[3] In 1881, Edward Brown founded another company in cooperation with the manufacturer of watch movements Louis Audemars, in Le Brassus, Switzerland, under the name Louis Audemars & Brown.[4] Clearly, this meant that Brown was sourcing movements from the Audemars factory. He had thus largely lost his ability to develop and manufacture watches and limited his activities to final assembly and sales in his Parisian jewellery store. This venture lasted only five years, however, and the bankruptcy of Louis Audemars in Switzerland put an end to it in 1886.[5] The legal form of the company is no longer known, but the Brown family continued to run a watchmaking workshop in Paris using the Breguet brand. It was a small business on a limited scale, linked to sales in its Paris boutique in the Opéra district.[6] The fate of this small company in the twentieth century is unknown. It moved to a new building in the neighbouring Rue de la Paix in 1933 but remained

Figure 6.1 Advertisement for Rolex using Breguet's Marie-Antoinette watch, 1953.

Source: *Eastern Jeweler and Watchmaker*, no. 17, 1953 © Archives Europa Star.

Note: Rolex used a Breguet watch in an advertising campaign to stress that its main innovation, the waterproof automatic chronometer, was a major step in the history of horology, like Abraham-Louis Breguet's creations at the end of the eighteenth century. Breguet was not a brand but a name that belonged to a shared history.

a small workshop.[7] The main activity documented is the development of a series of watches to meet demand from the French Air Force. In particular, it started to supply the wristwatch chronograph Type XX in 1954.[8] Breguet was not the only supplier, and production was outsourced to Mathey-Tissot & Cie SA, a small company based in Les Ponts-de-Martel, Switzerland, which used Valjoux calibers.[9] The orders from the air force did not lead to a change in the business model of the firm. This company was bought by the Chaumet jewellers in 1970, probably because there was no one in the Brown family to take it over.

When the brothers Jacques and Pierre Chaumet purchased this firm, their first objective was not to relaunch the Breguet brand but to acquire a workshop to assemble watches. Entering the watch retail business was one of their objectives at that time.[10] It was seen as a good opportunity to diversify their luxury jewellery collection. Consequently, in 1972, they engaged a young jeweller with experience in after-sale service for watches, François Bodet, and entrusted him with the creation and management of a jewellery watch store for their brand, Les Intemporelles Chaumet. The new store was opened in Paris in 1973 and offered a broad range of Swiss luxury watches, from Audemars Piguet and Chopard to Jaeger-LeCoultre and Rolex.[11] This diversification was the opportunity to reawaken the brand Breguet.

The Chaumet brothers had indeed asked Bodet to relaunch Breguet in the mid-1970s. The idea was to invest the profit from selling jewellery watches in the rebirth of this brand. When he started this new work, the only asset Bodet had was the brand itself.[12] In 1974, a new company, Chaumet SA, was founded in Geneva with a capital of 50,000 francs, for the trade of jewellery and watches.[13] Bodet developed a fruitful cooperation with museum curators, collectors, watch designer Gérald Genta and several watch suppliers introduced by the CEO of Vacheron Constantin. This made it possible to develop a few models of complicated mechanical watches in 1975 and 1976. To achieve this success, the internalization of technical knowledge was a first important step. In 1974, Bodet recruited Daniel Roth, a talented watchmaker who had worked for seven years at Audemars Piguet. Two years later, he became the technical director of the new Breguet workshop, re-opened in Le Brassus, Vallée de Joux, in Switzerland. Roth worked for this company until he established himself as an independent watchmaker in 1989.[14] Breguet was a true luxury startup, beginning its operation in a room hired in the Technical College of the Vallée de Joux until 1977, when it moved to the ground floor of a house.[15] Three years later, in 1980, a new company, Montres Breguet SA, was founded in Le Brassus with 400,000 francs in capital. The board of directors included Jacques and Pierre Chaumet, as well as three businessmen from Geneva.[16]

In order to re-establish the fame of Breguet in the market for luxury watches, Bodet needed to develop an impressive product that would attract the attention of afficionados and specialists of mechanical watchmaking. In particular, he decided to develop a wristwatch with a perpetual calendar, a complication that was very rare at that time.

Only a few pieces were realized as an investment in building a brand that embodied the watchmaking tradition. The company did not make any profit on it during the first years. The objective was to reawaken the Breguet brand. These watches were sold at first in the Place Vendôme boutique, and their price was set on purpose at twice the price of other brands.[17] It was a way of asserting both the luxurious character of Breguet watches, which accompanied the most famous watch brands in the shop windows, and its exceptionality, embodied by its price. In addition, this luxury strategy required that Breguet stop selling the chronograph Type XX. As some of these watches were in stock when Chaumet acquired Breguet in 1970, Bodet had at first thought to sell them. However, this product had a design that was too modern and a price point that was too low to fit with the new identity of the brand. It was seen as a potential damage, and consequently, it was necessary to stop its sale.[18]

The launch of a first series of watches went together with the publication of a book on Abraham-Louis Breguet and the organization of an exhibition in the International Watchmaking Museum in La Chaux-de-Fonds. *The Art of Breguet* was published in 1975 by the British artisan watchmaker George Daniels, who was already a respected authority on the technique of clocks and watches. This 400-page book is a seminal work on Breguet and was re-edited in 2021.[19] Daniels was also the author of a shorter catalogue of the exhibition organized in La Chaux-de-Fonds the following year.[20] These two events took place outside the influence of Chaumet. They appear to be the result of the work of George Daniels, who had an excellent relationship with the museum in La Chaux-de-Fonds. The idea was to honour a watchmaking genius of Swiss origin, at a time when the Swiss watchmaking industry was facing an existential crisis.[21] Moreover, François Bodet and Daniel Roth were in the very early stages of their work. They did not yet know what it would lead to. However, Daniels' book and the exhibition at the International Watchmaking Museum came at just the right time, as they gave academic legitimacy to the work undertaken by Chaumet, and the Parisian jeweller would develop cooperation with such actors in the 1980s.

During its first years of activity, in the late 1970s and early 1980s, Breguet's production was very small. It amounted to about 500–700 pieces a year, and half of them were sold to Chaumet's traditional consumers.[22] A new strategy was necessary to increase the customer base and to enter a phase of growth: the re-edition of old models of Abraham-Louis Breguet's watches as wristwatches (see Figure 6.2). The renaissance of mechanical watchmaking provided a favourable context, and this strategy made it possible to strengthen the link between the brand's famous origins and the present. The brand's historical heritage should not be confined to narratives but should be embodied in products. Daniel Roth and other watchmakers from La Vallée de Joux consequently developed a new series of watches. Breguet entered a period of growth between 1983 and 1987. The new strategy was epitomized by the decision, taken in 1987, to develop a tourbillon watch, as Breguet had been the inventor of this mechanism. In was launched in 1990 after three years of development.[23]

TO REMAIN FAITHFUL TO TRADITION

Three years' work for a Breguet watch

Abraham-Louis Breguet (1747-1823) was certainly one of the greatest watchmakers of all times. The horological industry owes him a considerable number of inventions which are still used today for certain top-quality mechanical models.

In so many years, his prestigious signature had gradually fallen into oblivion and while watch specialists and collectors still remembered the name of Breguet, there was no one to continue his work in our time. Reason therefore to be grateful to Messrs Chaumet, the famous jewellers of the Place Vendôme, Paris, who, besides reviving the Breguet name, retained its tradition and identity by creating a line of watches worthy of the prestigious models of the past. The work is carried out in Switzerland, in the Joux Valley where craftsmen are still found who are able to perpetuate the great traditions of the past with the same almost religious fervour for accuracy and perfection. The firm is managed with great competence by Mr François Bodet, while the production unit at Le Brassus has Mr Daniel Roth as technical manager.

A great tradition

The "Breguet style" — symbol of great technical and artistic refinement — is perpetuated therefore in the Le Brassus workshops in Switzerland. To show the will of the heads of this firm to remain entirely faithful to the tradition of the past, it is enough to say that today still, it takes them three years' work to make a great complication watch.

Figure 6.2 Advertisement for Breguet, 1983.

Source: *Europa Star Europe*, no. 142, 1983 (c) Archives Europa Star.

Note: The communication strategy of Breguet in the early 1980s consisted of stressing the maintenance of a technical heritage. The style of wristwatches was deeply inspired by the pocket watches developed by Abraham-Louis Breguet.

The heritage strategy adopted in 1983 was also embodied in new communication activities in order to transmit the values of the brand to a broader audience. Bodet and his staff understood the power of teaming up with museums and researchers.[24] Hence, not only did Breguet participate in the Basel Watch Fair for the first time in this year, it also presented its new collection to journalists in an event organized at the International Watchmaking Museum of La Chaux-de-Fonds.[25] Moreover, when André Curtit retired from his position as the curator of this institution in 1987, he was hired as a consultant for Breguet. He was, in particular, entrusted with the purchase of old Breguet watches from collectors and auctions, in order to develop their own collection of the brand – old models were an asset, as they were the basis for product development. He also produced certificates for the authentication of old watches.[26] In addition, Curtit's network among collectors and museums benefited the company. It was, for example, possible to gather old Breguet watches belonging to a large number of persons and institutions, and to set up in 1986 a small private exhibition in the boutiques of Chaumet around the world, from London to New York to Geneva.[27]

However, despite this strong business growth and a successful business model, Breguet abruptly changed owners in 1987. Chaumet's financial woes, marked by falling diamond prices and embezzlement by the company's directors, led to its bankruptcy.[28] A project of takeover by the jeweller Boucheron and the leather goods manufacturer Hermès was abandoned.[29] In July 1987, according to the Swiss press, the equity company Investcorp would have offered between 100 and 150 million FF (between 15 and 25 million USD at the time) to acquire the firm.[30] It purchased the company and separated it into two independent firms: Breguet, which was the only profitable business, and Chaumet, for the jewellery activities, which was drastically reorganized and recovered profitability only in 1998, before being sold the following year to LVMH for an undisclosed sum.[31] In Switzerland, Chaumet SA was closed and a new company, Société Nouvelle de Joaillerie Chaumet SA, was founded in Geneva in 1989 with a capital of 50,000 francs.[32] The activities of this firm are unknown but probably not related to jewellery. The headquarters were indeed transferred to Fribourg in 1992 and the company's name changed to Breguet Holding SA, with a capital raised to three million francs.[33] It was dissolved in 1996.[34] As for Montres Breguet SA, a new board of directors, including managers from Investcorp, was appointed in 1987.[35] François Bodet remained the executive director. Five years later, in 1992, he became president of the board.[36] The change of ownership had only a limited influence on the management of Montres Breguet SA during the first years. Bodet was the head of this business until 1996, and he ensured continuity in the development of the brand.

The brand's product development, based on the creation of wristwatches, directly inspired by old Breguet watches, and its marketing strategy continued in the same direction for a few years. In 1987, while Chaumet was bankrupted, the organization by Montres Breguet SA of a major watch exhibition in Le Louvre Museum in Paris was the best expression of this continuity. It gathered a selection of pieces from the sixteenth to the nineteenth centuries, many of them lent by the International Watchmaking Museum, which held the ambition to represent the development of the history of horology. This event was organized under the leadership of André Curtit, and the catalogue of the exhibition was prepared by art historian Catherine Cardinal, who would succeed Curtit at the head of the La Chaux-de-Fonds' museum in 1988, while Montres Breguet SA offered a financial support.[37] The *Europa Star* wrote that this catalogue would become 'a valuable document for watch collectors'.[38]

The cooperation with museums and auction companies continued in the years that followed, contributing to raising the awareness of the exceptionality of the Breguet brand among collectors. For example, in 1990, a public exhibition of 200 old Breguet watches was held at Hôtel des Bergues, one of the most exclusive hotels in Geneva. Then, it toured around the world before being auctioned in 1991. The role of Montres Breguet SA in this event is unclear, but the company was associated and offered an opportunity for collectors to subscribe to modern replicas of famous Breguet watches.[39] The same year, it launched a Breguet Prize of Contemporary Art (1991).[40] Breguet was not a mere watchmaker anymore: he would become the expression of European art.

These activities supported the growth of Breguet. The number of watches sold increased from 1,200 pieces in 1987 to 4,700 in 1993.[41] In 1991, the gross sales of the company amounted to 45 million dollars, and its profits reached 7 million.[42] However, this was not enough. Investcorp wanted to improve its profitability and make money rapidly. In 1992, it had planned to introduce 49 per cent of Breguet's capital to the Paris stock exchange.[43] This project was abandoned for unknown reasons, but it shows clearly the pressure from the new owner to increase profitability. Two main strategies were adopted in the 1990s to further develop the firm.

First, Investcorp invested massively in the production capacity and verticalized several operations to strengthen its autonomy.[44] In 1991, Montres Breguet SA purchased Société Anonyme Valdar, a small manufacturer of components for watches founded in L'Orient, in the Vallée de Joux, by Charles Meylan in 1918.[45] The following year, it took over Nouvelle Lemania SA, a company specializing in the development and production of chronographs and complicated mechanical movements.[46] The roots of this firm go back to the late nineteenth century. It was a major supplier of chronograph movements to numerous manufacturers during the first part of the twentieth century, including Omega, whose holding company, the Société Suisse pour l'Industrie Horlogère SA (SSIH), merged with it in 1932. However, following the dramatic financial problems faced by SSIH during the crisis, this firm had been disposed of in 1981 and became Nouvelle Lemania SA.[47] Finally, in 1994, Montres Breguet SA built a new manufacture in L'Abbaye, Vallée de Joux.[48] These developments were made possible by substantial capital injections, the source of which was undoubtedly Investcorp. In 1996, the capital of Montres Breguet SA amounted to six million francs, while it was only 400,000 francs a few years before.[49] The three companies were managed as a whole, sometimes called Groupe Horloger Breguet, but no company was registered under this name in Switzerland. Each of the three companies had an independent legal existence, although they all belonged to Investcorp.

Second, the management of Breguet adopted a new strategic objective to improve profitability: the launch of a second line of watches, made using standardized products and offered for a cheaper price. Most other traditional watch companies that exploit a historical name, as for Patek Philippe (see case no. 4), market a collection of simpler watches in order to increase their customer base and profits. Hence, in 1995, the management of Breguet decided to relaunch the chronograph Type XX, fifteen years after its decision to stop selling this product. The verticalization of Nouvelle Lemania supported this new objective. In 1997, the management of Breguet explained to the press that it targeted a decrease in the average prices and an increase in volume. This means that Breguet had to give less importance to the small series of highly complicated watches and more to the Classics and Type XX collections.[50] The first was used as an investment in maintaining the brand image, while the second enabled the brand to make money (see Figure 6.3).

Finally, the communication strategy remained the same as before. Breguet was the expression of a historical heritage, and the company continued to carry out various activities that embodied this message. In 1993, Bodet hired Emmanuel Breguet, a descendant of Abraham-Louis and a historian by training, as a consultant.[51] He published a historical book on his ancestor in 1997 and was still in the company in 2022, as head of patrimony.[52] In 1997, Montres Breguet SA also sponsored an exhibition on Abraham-Louis Breguet in the International Watchmaking Museum of La Chaux-de-Fonds, whose new curator was Catherine Cardinal.[53] The legitimacy conferred by museums and the academic world thus remained at the heart of the brand strategy.

The relaunch of XX Type chronograph was not very successful, at least during the first two years. In 1997, Breguet increased production to about 6,000 pieces, but gross sales amounted to only about 45 million francs.[54] The brand was unable to provide a satisfactory profit. Investcorp decided to give it up and find a buyer. This was a perfect opportunity for Swatch Group to strengthen its position in the segment of luxury watches. The takeover of Blancpain and the successful relaunch of Omega in the 1990s demonstrated the potential of the luxury watch market, provided an appropriate marketing strategy was implemented.[55] Breguet became a brand of Swatch Group in 1999. A new board of directors, including Nicolas G. Hayek (president), Jean-Claude Biver, Arlette Elsa Emch, Edgar Geiser, Georges N. Hayek junior and Hanspeter Rentsch, was appointed.[56] Nicolas Hayek himself took charge of the executive management of Breguet. He was chairman and CEO until 2010.

The evolution of Breguet since its takeover by Swatch Group can be clearly divided into two main phases (see Figure 6.4). There was first a period of fast growth, during

Figure 6.3 Report on Breguet, 1996.

Source: *Europa Star Europe*, no. 217, 1996 (c) Archives Europa Star.

Note: Highly complicated watches with a traditional design and the Type XX chronographs were the two faces of Breguet in the mid-1990s.

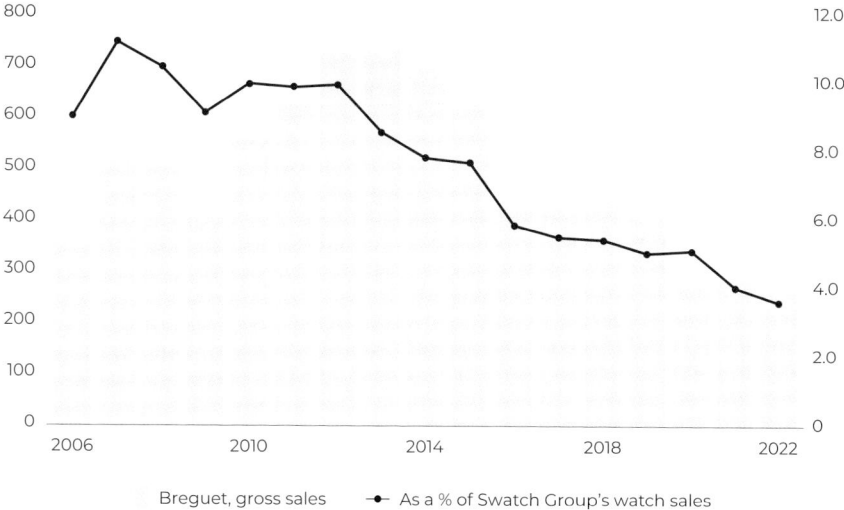

Figure 6.4 Gross sales of Montres Breguet SA, in million francs and as a percentage of Swatch Group's watch sales, 2006–22.

Source: Drafted by the authors on the base of Swatch Group, annual reports, 2006–22; Vontobel (2006–20) and Morgan Stanley (2021–2). Data unavailable before 2006.

which sales grew from probably 60 to 100 million francs, in 1999, to a peak of 720 to 725 million in 2012–13.[57] Breguet thus became a major brand of the group (about 10–11 per cent of watch sales in 2006–12). Next, there was a phase of a dramatic and continuous decline that has continued until today, despite the global expansion of the luxury market. In 2022, Breguet sales were estimated at 255 million francs. It represented only 3.6 per cent of watch sales by the group. Since 2020, Breguet has not been ranked within the top twenty largest Swiss watch brands by Morgan Stanley. This evolution undoubtedly reflects the impact of the anticorruption policy adopted by Xi Jinping, which had a dramatic impact on luxury business in China.[58] However, unlike other luxury watch brands, Breguet did not come back in the mid-2010s. The evolution of the brand over the last twenty-five years is hence not the sole result of external factors. Therefore, let us now focus on the management of the heritage of the brand.

After he took over the brand in 1999, Hayek adopted a strategy focused on the development of the production and retail capabilities of Breguet, as well as on massive investment in marketing. Nouvelle Lemania SA was enlarged in 2002 and stopped supplying customers outside of Swatch Group with mechanical movements the following year. In 2004, it was renamed Manufacture de Haute Horlogerie Breguet.[59] Moreover, like other brands in the luxury industry, Breguet developed its own network of mono-brand boutiques around the world. Their number went from only one in 2000 to twenty-two in 2010.[60] Hayek did not drastically change the heritage strategy of Breguet but emphasized a more focused message: Breguet was the expression of European classical culture. In the 2004 annual report of Swatch Group, he claimed that Breguet was 'the epitome of European culture and art'.[61] This declaration expressed a narrative that went beyond watchmaking, cultivating the imagery of an idealized European past. The bicentenary of the acquisition of a patent for a tourbillon in 2002 presented an opportunity to organize a mega-event at Château de Versailles, with customers, retailers and, of course, the press. Mozart was played to stress that Breguet was part of an exceptional environment.[62] Four years later, in 2006, a partnership was signed with Domaine de Marie-Antoinette at Versailles and Hayek was awarded the Médaille d'or de Grand Mécène de la Culture Française.[63] Montres Breguet SA engaged in the restoration of the estate of the domain. At the same time, the watchmakers of the company worked to create a replica of the watch made by Abraham-Louis Breguet for Marie-Antoinette. Considered as one of the world's most complicated watches, it had been stolen from a museum in Jerusalem in 1983 before being rediscovered in 2007, three years after Hayek decided to make a replica.[64] The new Marie-Antoinette watch was presented to the public at Baselworld in 2008.[65] It expressed perfectly the technical excellence of the brand and its relations with European aristocracy before the revolution. These historical roots were also at the heart of numerous exhibitions organized in cooperation with several museums around the world, including the Heritage Museum in Saint-Petersburg (2004) and Le Louvre Museum in Paris (2009).[66]

However, while the marketing message of Breguet was clearly focused on the contribution of this brand to European classical culture, Hayek adopted an ambiguous strategy regarding product diversification. On the one hand, besides the pursuit of the development of complicated wristwatches inspired by old watches made by Breguet himself, he launched in 2002 a new collection of ladies' watches, named Queen of Naples, in reference to a watch created for Caroline Murat between 1801 and 1812. This product fitted perfectly within the heritage strategy pursued over the years. On the other hand, he continued the exploitation of the second brand's Type XX, developed in several new versions, in order to increase profit, although the narrative around this second brand is unrelated to European classical culture. The relative importance in the gross sales of classical luxury watches and of the chronograph Type XX is unknown, so it is impossible to properly estimate the main driver of the fast growth of sales between 2000 and 2012. Finally, one must mention that Breguet also developed a collection of jewellery in 2000. The impact of such diversification is not clear, but it was undoubtedly not a success. The brand Breguet was never ranked among the world's top-largest sixty jewellery brands in the reports of the consulting company Euromonitor between 2009 and 2018.[67]

In 2010, after Nicolas Hayek died, his grandson Marc A. Hayek was appointed chairman and CEO of the brand. During the first years, product development continued on a similar basis (complicated wristwatches as a modern version of old models and innovation in mechanical watchmaking). The new watches created were acclaimed by the profession. Breguet was awarded the Aiguille d'Or at the Grand Prix d'Horlogerie de Genève (GPHG) in 2014.

However, the first signs of change regarding the brand's position soon appeared. The concept of the embeddedness of European classical culture was diluted, step by step. Breguet started to engage in a broad range of partnerships and global events – but without a clear and exclusive link with its heritage. It continued to cooperate with Le Louvre Museum (2014) and organized a Marie-Antoinette exhibition in Tokyo (2016), but these sponsoring activities had become less visible within a general marketing strategy that lost its relevance to the heritage of the brand.[68] Sponsoring was not as strongly related to classical culture as it had been until 2010. For example, it included a partnership with an Italian museum for an exhibition about Kandinsky, the founder of abstract art, in 2017.[69] The following year, Breguet became a partner of the Race for Water, a private foundation that acts for preserving water and struggles against plastic pollution in oceans.[70] Finally, in the same period, the company launched the Breguet Classic Tour, based on the concept of the lifestyle of a gentleman. This was related to the use of Winston Churchill, a customer of Breguet, as a leading figure for advertisement in the UK, then globally, after 2016.[71]

Moreover, the global market for luxury watches changed after 2010 with the increasing popularity of sports watches. The challenge, well understood by companies like Audemars Piguet and Patek Philippe, was to offer more affordable products that embodied the core values of the brand and were perfectly integrated in their core narrative. From this perspective, the chronograph Type XX, available in several new models after 2010, continued to present major weaknesses due to the lack of continuity with the classical complicated watches.

The increasing distance between the watches created by Breguet and the message diffused to consumers through marketing activities led to a dilution of the brand value. The clear heritage built up by Nicolas Hayek, which intimately linked the Breguet brand to European classical culture, has gradually disintegrated. The fall in sales is clearly an expression of this change. The management of the firm reacted by abandoning the jewellery collection – since 2017, Breguet jewellery has disappeared from annual reports. Four years later, in 2021, Marc A. Hayek withdrew from the position of CEO – although he is still chairman – and appointed Lionel a Marca, a watchmaker with nearly thirty years of experience in Swatch Group.[72]

Case 9: British watch masters

Although several British artisan watchmakers played a major role in the technical development of the clock and watch industry during the seventeenth and eighteenth centuries, their firms vanished during the second part of the nineteenth century. Clustered in London, these artisans focused on the creation and manufacture of high-quality watches using traditional techniques. However, their choice not to use modern manufacturing machinery and methods led to the decline of their competitiveness – and ultimately the disappearance of their firms.[73] Hence, the watchmaking industry is virtually absent from the United Kingdom today. However, in the 1990s, with the emergence of luxury mechanical watchmaking based on the exploitation of a historical tradition, the names of the great British artisan watchmakers of the past attracted new interest. Exploiting their heritage offered the prospect of potential commercial success. For the most part, it was Swiss rather than British entrepreneurs who seized these opportunities.

In 1994, Eric Loth, an engineer and former manager in Société Suisse de Microélectronique et d'Horlogerie (SMH, Swatch Group since 1998), and Pierre-André Finazzi, a watch designer who had notably worked for Corum, Ebel and Piaget, teamed up to create their own business.[74] They purchased six names of British clock and watchmakers: Arnold & Son, Earnshaw, Graham, Mudge, Quare and Tompion.[75] The next year, they founded a firm, Les Monts SA, in La Chaux-de-Fonds.[76] They benefited from the cooperation with Ernst Thomke, who invested in their firm and undoubtedly offered valuable support.[77] Thomke had been the head of ETA and later of the watchmaking division of SMH. He left SMH in 1991, after a conflict with Nicolas G. Hayek, and pursued his career in various industrial firms.[78] Investing in Les Monts SA was part of a personal strategy to come back in the watch industry. In addition, he was a member of the board of Montres Davidoff SA, a small firm founded in Fribourg in 1988, and an advisor for watchmaking in the Sandoz Foundation, the major investor of Parmigiani Fleurier.[79] During the second part of the 1990s, Les Monts SA continued to register several brands related to British clock and watch history, particularly Marine Timekeeper Arnold & Sons (1997), Masters of the Longitude (1998), Arnold & Dent (1999), Arnold & Frodsham (1999) and Graham (1999).[80]

At the same time, Les Monts SA selected three brands that seemed the most promising: Thomas Tompion (1639–1713), George Graham (1673/75–1751) and John Arnold (1736–99), who founded Arnold & Son in 1787.[81] All of them had been elite artisans engaged in creating high-quality clocks and marine chronometers. The wristwatches developed had to be a tribute to their contribution to the history of horology. They designed high-precision complicated watches for the brands Tompion and Graham, and a watch inspired by marine chronometers for the third, as Arnold had been actively engaged in developing such instruments. This first collection of watches

Creating New Brands from Heritage

was presented at the Basel Fair in 1996 as 'The British Masters of Timekeeping'.[82] It was brought to markets in Europe, the US and (later) Asia.

Design is not only a matter of style. Launching watches as a tribute to the heritage of the great artisan watchmakers of the past requires one to provide a unique product to consumers. It was therefore necessary to develop specific high-quality mechanical movements that would embody the heritage. Loth and Finazzi outsourced this production to Jaquet. This company, which specialized in the manufacture of complicated mechanical movements for assembly makers, had been founded by Jean-Pierre Jaquet, a former employee of watch company Aubry Frères SA.[83] In 1990, he left this firm and founded in La Chaux-de-Fonds his own enterprise specializing in the manufacture of complicated watches, Jaquet Baume SA.[84] The comeback of mechanical watches and the foundation of several new businesses launched in this new segment indicated a potential business opportunity. The business model relied on the use of ETA movements to develop watch complications.[85] Renamed Manufacture La Joux Perret SA in 2004, following Jaquet's epic arrest for gold theft and counterfeiting activities, this company had been the supplier of not only Les Monts SA but of other important manufactures, like Girard Perregaux SA, which used a chronograph developed for Graham for watches made for its partner Ferrari.[86]

As discussed above regarding successful cases such as Blancpain and Breguet, storytelling is a core issue when launching heritage watches. Claiming these products are the expression of the excellence of the watchmaking tradition is not enough. Specific actions must accompany the narratives. This was somehow a weakness of Les Monts during the first years. The company was focused on the products and did not give much importance to storytelling. Hence, in May 1999, the company sent a box containing three watches by Arnolds & Son, Graham and Tompion to an auction organized in New York by Antiquorum. It was, however, unable to sell them.[87] Attracting the attention of the public and collectors was a necessary condition.

A new strategy was needed to ensure the growth of these brands. Loth decided to give more importance to the British market, which had been neglected until then, considering the identity of his brands. A new investor, William Asprey, owner of a renowned luxury watch retailer in London, William & Son, invested in the business and joined the board of directors in 2000.[88] At the same time, the company changed its name and became The British Masters SA (BM), the official objective of which was 'to exploit in particular the trademarks of English master watchmakers of the seventeenth and eighteenth centuries of which it is the owner, to draw inspiration from their designs and to refer to them in its production'.[89] BM refocused on two brands – Arnold & Son and Graham – and continued to develop highly complicated wristwatches, targeting the London market.[90] La Joux Perret SA, in which Eric Loth had invested personally, remained the main supplier, but BM also cooperated with renamed independent artisan watchmakers, like Christophe Claret, to develop specific movements.[91] Moreover, being offered together with François-Paul Journe and Audemars Piguet watches in the William & Son boutique dramatically increased the visibility and value of the Arnold & Son and Graham brands. The emphasis on the United Kingdom was finally reflected in the outfits of CEO Eric Loth, who started wearing bowler hats and English suits to watchmaking events.[92]

As for Finazzi, he left BM in 2001 and founded a new company in La Chaux-de-Fonds the following year, Ellicott SA.[93] While working as a designer for independent watch brands like Perrelet,[94] he developed his own business based on similar principles that he had learnt at Les Monts SA: launching heritage watches as a tribute to a famous British clockmaker of the past. His new target was John Ellicott (1706–72), who had been a clockmaker of the king.[95] Finazzi registered the brand in 2001.[96] He cooperated again with Christophe Claret, to whom was outsourced the creation and production of an automatic tourbillon equipped with two rotors.[97] His collections were presented for the first time at Basel World in 2010. One of the niche segments targeted by this brand was complicated mechanical watches for women.[98] However, the relation with the heritage of Ellicott was rather vague, and this new brand was unable to make a place for itself in the extremely competitive market for new independent brands of highly complicated timepieces. In 2019, Ellicott SA was liquidated.[99]

In 2010, BM was reorganized. It was probably too difficult for a small company to properly manage two different brands at the same time. Hence, BM sold Arnold & Son to some investors close to the movement producer Manufacture La Joux Perret SA. They organized a separate company to manage this brand. In 2012, Arnold & Son was acquired by the Japanese group Citizen Watch when it took over the holding company controlling La Joux Perret, and it still belongs to it today.[100] Its proximity with a producer of complicated mechanical movements and integration within a multinational enterprise provided both the know-how and capital to ensure the development of the brand. Arnold & Son continued to develop highly complicated watches and engaged in a cooperation with specialized artisans for decoration, notably for engraving and miniature painting (see Figure 6.5).[101]

BM consequently refocused on a single brand, Graham, and the company was renamed Graham SA in 2010.[102] Pursuing a business model based on its cooperation with independent watch designers and manufacturers of movements, this company continued in the development of highly complicated watches. In 2012, the CEO argued that his brand was 'so British in style and so Swiss in technique'.[103] Although this statement is rather vague, it justified the fact that Graham was not following the designs of the eighteenth century (see Figure 6.6). It launched colourful, sometimes flashy, sports watches, chronographs and tourbillons positioned in an exclusive segment. The tourbillon Geo Graham The Moon, launched in 2013, had a retail price of 240,000 francs.[104] The case of Graham embodies perfectly the role played by independent suppliers in the development of heritage brands. In 2014, Eric Loth testified:

96 MECHANICAL WONDERS · ARNOLD & SON europa star

The Symbiosis of Time

After lengthy and meticulous research, the True North Perpetual by Arnold & Son represents a landmark in contemporary watchmaking.

D evised by Eric A. Loth, the CEO of British Masters, the True North Perpetual complication reflects a symbiosis of time, within which civil time, i.e. the average time within a time zone and the globe as a cosmic clock are brought together for the first time in an extraordinary wristwatch.

Powered by a hand wound movement with a 7-day power reserve, the watch features a perpetual calendar which takes account of leap years, a moon phase display calculated on a 29.5 day lunar cycle, a 24-hour time zone indication which can also show the mean solar time, and a double equation of time display (equation segment and running equation indication, both giving the difference between true solar time and mean solar time).

The True North Perpetual is the very first timepiece capable of indicating true solar time in a given place and the true geographical North – once a day at true solar noon. It also includes another innovation: it incorporates summer time or daylight saving time correction and the longitude of a given location.

Crafted in 18 carat white gold the True North Perpetual is equipped with a movement produced exclusively by Jaquet SA for Arnold & Son. Using a revolutionary technology of gears with an elastic toothing, the movement is also equipped with a three-level going-train comprising an interior toothing (patented). The finely decorated movement features the '1764' signature on one of the wheel bars. Water-resistant to 30 metres, this handsomely innovative timepiece is also available in a Limited Edition in platinum and a pink gold version featuring a progressive minute-track. ⟨ (DML)

For further information related to this brand, click on Brand Index at www.europastar.com

Figure 6.5 Report on Arnold & Son, 2005.

Source: *Europa Star Europe*, no. 270, 2005 (c) Archives Europa Star.

Note: This model of highly complicated wristwatch perfectly illustrates the weak link between the historical heritage of Arnold & Son, a company specializing in marine chronometry, and the contemporary products developed in its honour.

Graham in the moon

GEO.GRAHAM THE MOON by Graham

There is an impressive piece on show at Graham: the Geo.Graham The Moon. A flying tourbillon shares room on the blue dial with an enormous high-precision, hand-pained retrograde moon phase. In theory, the display only needs adjusting every 122 years (by simply pressing a corrector) and respects the synodic period, which corresponds to 29 days, 12 hours, 44 minutes and 2.9 seconds precisely, if not to the second then to the nearest minute. Pushing the celestial metaphor further, Graham has dotted the dial with 45 diamonds to represent the main constellations spread around the epicentre of the watch, the pivot for the hands, which represents the position of the North star, the brightest polar star in the Ursa Minor constellation.

The piece is finished off by a painted sapphire bezel that depicts the Milky Way as seen through a telescope.

George Graham regularly observed the moon at the start of the 18th century (from Fleet Street, which would be impossible today) and would no doubt appreciate this tribute. And it is a rare (20 pieces) and costly (CHF 240,000) tribute. ❮

For more information about Graham click on Brand Index at www.europastar.com

Figure 6.6 Report on Graham, 2013.
Source: *Europa Star Europe*, no. 318, 2013 (c) Archives Europa Star.
Note: Graham has focused on the creation of highly complicated watches with modern designs. Here also, the relation with the historical heritage linked to the name is rather vague.

As long as independent movement manufacturers exist in Switzerland, they will represent the best option for an independent brand like Graham to realize specific projects on order with their complete scale of manufacturing capability. Thanks to such access of diversified production sources, Graham could realize very ambitious movement concept such as the Tourbillon Orrery Planetarium, the Silverstone RS Skeleton or the Endurance Chronograph movement concept.[105]

However, despite the survival of Arnold & Son and Graham for more than two decades, neither of these brands had been able to establish themselves among the annual rankings of the top fifty largest Swiss watch brands established by Morgan Stanley since 2018.[106] According to an estimate by a Swiss newspaper, the gross sales of each brand amounted to about 30 million francs in 2008.[107] It obviously has not developed much, even to the present day.

Case 10: JeanRichard

The examples of Breguet and of the British watch artisans show that launching heritage brands had become highly popular in the Swiss watch industry following the 1990s. Other examples would include Ferdinand Berthoud, Jaquet Droz, Leroy, Louis Moinet and James Pellaton. The fortunes of these brands are varied, with some establishing themselves as major players in contemporary luxury watchmaking, despite the difficulties (Breguet), while others struggled to find a business model that would allow them to grow (British watch masters). There is no need to discuss all of these heritage brands. However, it is worth taking one more example – that of JeanRichard – because of the legendary importance of this name.

The name refers to Daniel JeanRichard (c. 1665–1741), a watchmaker who worked in Le Locle and is considered to be the father of watchmaking in the Neuchâtel mountains. Since the nineteenth century, he has acquired the stature of a quasi-heroic figure. He embodies the creative genius and resilience of Swiss watchmakers.[108] The uniqueness of this character clearly makes him an excellent target for the launch of a heritage brand as a tribute to the founding father of the industry. However, attempts to use this name have been relatively disappointing to date.

Although some watch companies were named Jeanrichard SA, in Le Locle and in Geneva during the middle of the twentieth century, they had nothing to do with the exploitation of the legendary figure of Daniel JeanRichard to build a heritage brand. This name was used as the patronym of the family of the owners of these firms. In 1961, the company Jeanrichard SA, in Geneva, even changed its name to Aquastar SA, which expressed better its objective to specialize in diving and sports watches.[109] Hence, in 1983, this company used the brand Jeanrichard for some watches, but without any link to a heritage strategy. According to a press release, this collection 'comprises sports and city watches of elegant design but exceptionally water resistant and dependable. These models are available in steel, bicolour, chromed black.'[110]

The real use of the brand JeanRichard to develop a heritage strategy goes back to 1988 when Jean Moro, a truculent businessman involved in a number of financial affairs and close to the jet-setting milieu of French-speaking Switzerland, founded Jeanrichard SA in Geneva, in the offices of the company Métropolitain Fiduciaire SA.[111] The capital of the company amounted to 150,000 francs, of which 100,000 francs were used to purchase the brand JeanRichard from Nouvelle Lémania SA, which had purchased it from Aquastar in 1986.[112] Everything seems to indicate that the directors of Nouvelle Lémania wanted to launch their own brand. Biver experienced significant success with Blancpain at that time and attracted the attention of other enterprises. However, for unknown reasons, they abandoned this project. A few months later, Moro sold Jeanrichard SA to Jean-Paul Corbaz, who moved it to Le Brassus, in the Vallée de Joux, about three kilometres from Nouvelle Lemania.[113] Jean-Claude Grenier, a former member of the board of Nouvelle Lemania, was appointed director of Jeanrichard SA.[114] It is not clear what Corbaz's objective was, nor whom he worked for, but he probably used a financial intermediary from Geneva to hide the purchase of the brand. No watch was properly developed during this period. Corbaz, who had been engaged in a large number of financial and real estate businesses in Switzerland, was undoubtedly looking for a partner with whom he could relaunch the brand. In 1993, he was appointed a board member of Girard Perregaux SA, in La Chaux-de-Fonds, and the following year, Jeanrichard SA moved to this city, at the same address as Girard Perreaux.[115] It was taken over two years later by the owner of Girard Perregaux, the Italian businessman Luigi Macaluso, who became chairman, while Corbaz remained as a member of the board.[116] Grenier left the company that year.[117] The company also registered the brand Daniel JeanRichard.

Macaluso's objective was to use Daniel JeanRichard as a second brand for his company Girard-Perregaux. In 1997, he explained to the press that he would launch a collection of steel watches and market a first batch of 1,000–1,500 pieces.[118] At the same time, Girard-Perregaux experienced a dramatic move up in the market. It had transformed itself into a luxury brand that embodied the quintessence of the Swiss watchmaking tradition. Macaluso developed a modernized version of the Golden Bridge model, developed as a pocket watch in the middle of the nineteenth century, and started a cooperation with Ferrari. In this context, Daniel JeanRichard had a specific role to fulfil. In 1998, Macaluso explained his strategy for this brand:

> It was born of a very clear idea: to offer a product consistent with its price/quality ratio, without fictional added-value but intended for a sophisticated target public. … With Daniel JeanRichard, we want to reach a very modern clientele, that cultural and social niche of intellectually refined individuals who don't want to spend a lot of money on a watch and don't want to flaunt their purchasing power.[119]

Prices were set up between 400 and 1500 francs.[120]

However, there was no relation between the name JeanRichard and the identity of watches launched under this brand. Macaluso used quartz movements, marketed various types of watches (including chronographs) and followed fashionable trends. For example, JeanRichard made watches with very large dials when there was a demand for this kind of product (Grand TV Screen model, see Figure 6.7). Despite the possession of a legendary name, no heritage was created for the brand. It is true that it would have been difficult to develop a discourse on JeanRichard's historical tradition without damaging Girard-Perregaux, which was positioned precisely as a heritage brand. The challenge was to sell watches that were accessible to a clientele that was different from, and complementary to, Girard-Perregaux, and not to launch watches that were similar to Girard-Perregaux but less expensive.

The company's management was aware of these difficulties and of the need to make better use of the JeanRichard brand. Hence, in 2003, it launched a tourbillon watch for its second brand, which surprised even the watch-specialized press.[121] The following year, in 2004, it developed a manufacture movement, JR1000.[122] These innovations were followed by a major increase in prices. JeanRichard was clearly repositioned as a luxury brand. In 2010, the price range was between 7,000 and 10,000 francs.[123]

This change was part of the merger between Sowind Group, founded in 1988 by Macaluso as the parent company of Girard-Perregaux, and the French luxury

Figure 6.7 Grand TV Screen developed by JeanRichard, 2003.
Source: *Europa Star Europe*, no. 259, 2003 © Archives Europa Star.

Figure 6.8 Advertisement for JeanRichard, 2008.

Source: *Europa Star Russia*, no. 16, 2008 © Archives Europa Star.

Note: The partnership between the Sowind group, owner of JeanRichard, and the French luxury conglomerate PPR (Kering) led to an attempt to move the JeanRichard brand upmarket. The experiment was short-lived.

conglomerate PPR (Kering since 2013). The latter acquired a 23 per cent stake in Sowind in 2008.[124] After PPR acquired the majority of the capital, in 2011, the reposition to luxury took a step further.[125] The French conglomerate appointed Michele Sofisti, a former manager in Swatch Group and LVMH, as the new CEO of Sowind. He decided to completely change the position of JeanRichard, with a 'very identifiable look' and a cheaper price point of between 2500 and 4000 francs.[126] The new target was a large market of accessible luxury, with watches equipped with ETA movements. However, here too, no heritage linking the brand to the historical origins of Swiss watchmaking had been built (see Figure 6.8). The few historical models launched were even part of Girard-Perregaux's past and not the legend of Daniel JeanRichard, which added to the confusion. For example, in 2014, JeanRichard launched a special model as a tribute to the 150th anniversary of diplomatic relations between Switzerland and Japan, in 2014: François Perregaux, a member of the Girard Perregaux family, was the first Swiss watchmaker established in Japan.[127] The repositioning implemented by Sofisti was not successful. When Antonio Calce, a former manager in Richemont group and former CEO of Corum Watches, was appointed as the new CEO of Sowind in 2015, he declared that he wanted to redefine the identity and position of JeanRichard, on the basis of 'a more limited number of models and a more clearly-defined scope'.[128] However, this brand has been put on the back burner, with Sowind focusing on the management of Girard-Perregaux and a second luxury brand, Ulysse Nardin, acquired by Kering in 2014. In 2022, Kering sold the Sowind group to its management. It is again independent and remains focused on its two main brands, with JeanRichard staying dormant.

Case 11: Heritage brands with a technical foundation: Czapek, Lowenthal and Pouzait

The brands discussed in the previous three cases were basically founded on a heritage that took inspiration from the personality and the life of famous artisan watchmakers of the past. Much more than the creations themselves, the fantasy world created around the reawakened watchmakers is at the heart of these brands' narratives. Breguet may be the exception, with the relaunch of wristwatches inspired by the master's earlier creations, but this brand has had its heyday as the embodiment of European classical art.

To conclude this discussion of heritage watch brands, we will focus on a few cases of brands whose heritage has a strong technical foundation. These are small, independent brands that have been relaunched in the last ten years by Harry Guhl.[129] Despite their size, these companies and startups shed light on the way in which new companies exploiting a technical heritage are created.

Guhl was working in the art world when he became interested in reviving vanished brands – he had been an art gallery owner, a global head of VIP relations at Art Basel and an art consultant for Rolls-Royce Motorcars. By 2023, he had registered and reawakened a total of seventeen watch brands. The business model was to create a legal framework related to a watchmaker or inactive watch company, transform it into a brand and sell it to investors. The discussion below is based on three brands: Czapek, Lowenthal and Pouzait.

Czapek is undoubtedly the most successful brand relaunched by Guhl. In early 2012, he registered this brand and managed it through a company he had founded the year before, Lissignol SA. The trademark Lissignol was sold to Universal Genève, and the company was renamed Czapek & Cie SA.[130] The company had an initial capital of 100,000 francs. Guhl produced a first batch of less than twenty chronographs, using vintage Valjoux calibres that were completely reworked. He had been in contact with the suppliers directly, ordering all parts and giving them to a watchmaker to assemble them into a watch. The idea was to make the brand more feasible for investors, as well as strengthen the trademark while giving possible brand managers a better understanding of the high potential offered by Czapek. The brand refers indeed to Franciszek Czapek (or François Czapek), a watchmaker of Polish origin, born in 1811 and established in Geneva in 1832. He was a business partner of Antoni Patek, with whom he owned and managed Patek, Czapek & Co. between 1839 and 1845, before starting his own company.[131] Czapek produced original watches and was a supplier to the imperial court during the French Second Empire. Some of his watches had reappeared after 2000 in auctions organized by Antiquorum and attracted the attention of collectors.

In order to manage his new business, Guhl looked for a CEO. He started to work with Xavier de Roquemaurel, a former manager of luxury fashion brands who had moved to watchmaking three years before (he had been in charge of brand marketing for Ebel until 2012). In 2014, he became a shareholder and took over the management of Czapek & Cie as a CEO. The objective was to launch an independent *haute horlogerie* brand. During the first years, his work focused on the establishment of the heritage of François Czapek, through commissioned research by a historian, and the development of a concept to create a wristwatch. Guhl and de Roquemaurel were joined by Sébastien Follonier, a watchmaker specializing in complicated watches who had been employed by several companies of La Chaux-de-Fonds, including Girard Perregaux SA, Greubel & Forsey and Corum. The company then developed through equity crowdfunding. The clients of the brand became investors and supported its development.

The three horological entrepreneurs needed an emblematic watch to relaunch Czapek. They wanted to start their business with a tribute to Franciszek Czapek. Their attention focused on a pocket watch made in around 1850, with power reserve, two barrels and tandem winding, sold by Antiquorum in 2005 (now in Czapek ownership).[132] The idea was to develop a modern version as a wristwatch. This was made possible thanks to independent suppliers based in Switzerland. The new proprietary movement was designed in collaboration with Jean-François Mojon, from Chronode, a small company founded in 2005 that specialized in the design of watch movements.[133] He had already developed several high complication watches for independent brands and manufacturers. External parts were notably provided by Neo-Desis (design), AB Product (case) and Donzé Cadrans (dial).[134] Despite the general trend of the verticalization of suppliers in the watch industry since the late 1990s, maintaining a dense network of small, independent companies specialized in the making of high-quality components, mostly in small batches, made it possible to source all necessary parts to produce the first Czapek wristwatch. It was presented to the public at Baselworld in 2016. Although Czapek & Cie was able to sell only one watch during this event, sales increased during the year and reached a total of eighty-eight watches by the end of December.[135] In the meanwhile, Czapek won the public prize at the Grand Prix d'Horlogerie de Genève (GPHG) in November, which boosted the visibility of the new brand.

Having established the reputation of the brand on the basis of a technical heritage that was recognized by the watch milieu, the owners took more liberty in developing new models. Czapek & Cie has hence continued its growth through its cooperation with the watchmaking ecosystem, co-developing *haute horlogerie* models with independent suppliers (see Figure 6.9). It became profitable in 2018 and kept its business model focused on providing a niche for collectors (production between 100 and 1,000 watches a year, with an average price of 18,000 francs in 2019).[136] In 2020, the launch of the Antarctique model, positioned in the popular segment of luxury sports watches, contributed to the stable growth of the company. Guhl resigned from his position as a president of the board in 2022, although he remains the largest shareholder.

In the meantime, Guhl had developed a project to relaunch the Lowenthal brand. He had been collecting such watches for many years and had the opportunity to purchase old calibres and components. In 2016, he registered the brand.[137] Although there is a small quantity of Lowenthal wristwatches dating from the 1930s and 1940s, no information has been found on the brand itself or the company owning it. Watches are mostly chronographs, some of them being supplied to fashion companies like

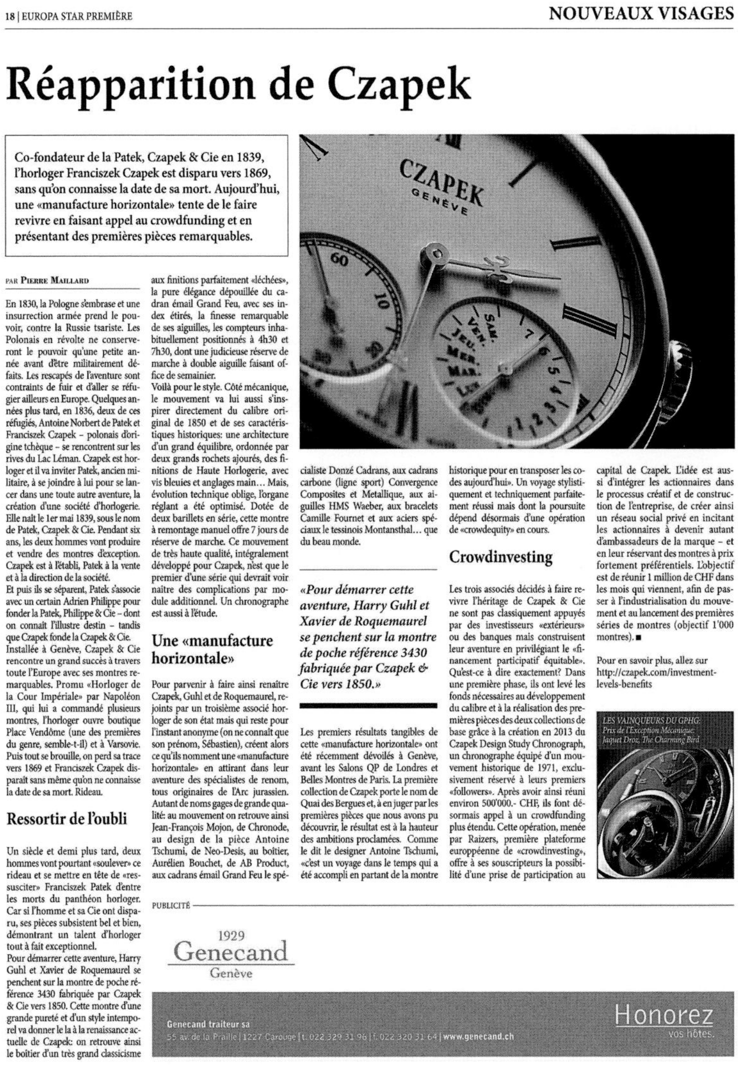

18 | EUROPA STAR PREMIÈRE NOUVEAUX VISAGES

Réapparition de Czapek

Co-fondateur de la Patek, Czapek & Cie en 1839, l'horloger Franciszek Czapek est disparu vers 1869, sans qu'on connaisse la date de sa mort. Aujourd'hui, une «manufacture horizontale» tente de le faire revivre en faisant appel au crowdfunding et en présentant des premières pièces remarquables.

PAR PIERRE MAILLARD

En 1830, la Pologne s'embrase et une insurrection armée prend le pouvoir, contre la Russie tsariste. Les Polonais en révolte ne conserveront le pouvoir qu'une petite année avant d'être militairement défaits. Les rescapés de l'aventure sont contraints de fuir et d'aller se réfugier ailleurs en Europe. Quelques années plus tard, en 1836, deux de ces réfugiés, Antoine Norbert de Patek et Franciszek Czapek – polonais d'origine tchèque – se rencontrent sur les rives du Lac Léman. Czapek est horloger et il va inviter Patek, ancien militaire, à se joindre à lui pour se lancer dans une toute autre aventure, la création d'une société d'horlogerie. Elle naît le 1er mai 1839, sous le nom de Patek, Czapek & Cie. Pendant six ans, les deux hommes vont produire et vendre des montres d'exception. Czapek est à l'établi, Patek à la vente et à la direction de la société.

Et puis ils se séparent, Patek s'associe avec un certain Adrien Philippe pour fonder la Patek, Philippe & Cie – dont on connaît l'illustre destin – tandis que Czapek fonde la Czapek & Cie.

Installée à Genève, Czapek & Cie rencontre un grand succès à travers toute l'Europe avec ses montres remarquables. Promu «Horloger de la Cour Impériale» par Napoléon III, qui lui a commandé plusieurs montres, l'horloger ouvre boutique Place Vendôme (une des premières du genre, semble-t-il) et à Varsovie. Puis tout se brouille, on perd sa trace vers 1869 et Franciszek Czapek disparaît sans même qu'on ne connaisse la date de sa mort. Rideau.

Ressortir de l'oubli

Un siècle et demi plus tard, deux hommes vont pourtant «soulever» ce rideau et se mettre en tête de «ressusciter» Franciszek Patek d'entre les morts du panthéon horloger. Car si l'homme et sa Cie ont disparu, ses pièces subsistent bel et bien, démontrant un talent d'horloger tout à fait exceptionnel.

Pour démarrer cette aventure, Harry Guhl et Xavier de Roquemaurel se penchent sur la montre de poche référence 3430 fabriquée par Czapek & Cie vers 1850. Cette montre d'une grande pureté et d'un style intemporel va donner le la à la renaissance actuelle de Czapek: on retrouve ainsi le boîtier d'un très grand classicisme aux finitions parfaitement «léchées», la pure élégance dépouillée du cadran émail Grand Feu, avec ses index étirés, la finesse remarquable de ses aiguilles, les compteurs inhabituellement positionnés à 4h30 et 7h30, dont une judicieuse réserve de marche à double aiguille faisant office de semainier.

Voilà pour le style. Côté mécanique, le mouvement va lui aussi s'inspirer directement du calibre original de 1850 et de ses caractéristiques historiques: une architecture d'un grand équilibre, ordonnée par deux grands rochets ajourés, des finitions de Haute Horlogerie, avec vis bleuies et anglages main… Mais, évolution technique oblige, l'organe réglant a été optimisé. Dotée de deux barillets en série, cette montre à remontage manuel offre 7 jours de réserve de marche. Ce mouvement de très haute qualité, intégralement développé pour Czapek, n'est que le premier d'une série qui devrait voir naître des complications par module additionnel. Un chronographe est aussi à l'étude.

Une «manufacture horizontale»

Pour parvenir à faire ainsi renaître Czapek, Guhl et de Roquemaurel, rejoints par un troisième associé horloger de son état mais qui reste pour l'instant anonyme (on ne connaît que son prénom, Sébastien), créent alors ce qu'ils nomment une «manufacture horizontale» en attirant dans leur aventure des spécialistes de renom, tous originaires de l'Arc jurassien. Autant de noms gages de grande qualité: au mouvement on retrouve ainsi Jean-François Mojon, de Chronode, au design de la pièce Antoine Tschumi, de Neo-Desis, au boîtier, Aurélien Bouchet, de AB Product, aux cadrans émail Grand Feu le spécialiste Donzé Cadrans, aux cadrans carbone (ligne sport) Convergence Composites et Metallique, aux aiguilles HMS Waeber, aux bracelets Camille Fournet et aux aciers spéciaux le tessinois Montansthal… que du beau monde.

«Pour démarrer cette aventure, Harry Guhl et Xavier de Roquemaurel se penchent sur la montre de poche référence 3430 fabriquée par Czapek & Cie vers 1850.»

Les premiers résultats tangibles de cette «manufacture horizontale» ont été récemment dévoilés à Genève, avant les Salons QP de Londres et Belles Montres de Paris. La première collection de Czapek porte le nom de Quai des Bergues et, à en juger par les premières pièces que nous avons pu découvrir, le résultat est à la hauteur des ambitions proclamées. Comme le dit le designer Antoine Tschumi, «c'est un voyage dans le temps qui a été accompli en partant de la montre historique pour en transposer les codes aujourd'hui». Un voyage stylistiquement et techniquement parfaitement réussi mais dont la poursuite dépend désormais d'une opération de «crowdequity» en cours.

Crowdinvesting

Les trois associés décidés à faire revivre l'héritage de Czapek & Cie ne sont pas classiquement appuyés par des investisseurs «extérieurs» ou des banques mais construisent leur aventure en privilégiant le «financement participatif équitable». Qu'est-ce à dire exactement? Dans une première phase, ils ont levé les fonds nécessaires au développement du calibre et à la réalisation des premières pièces des deux collections de base grâce à la création en 2013 du Czapek Design Study Chronograph, un chronographe équipé d'un mouvement historique de 1971, exclusivement réservé à leurs premiers «followers». Après avoir ainsi réuni environ 500'000.- CHF, ils font désormais appel à un crowdfunding plus étendu. Cette opération, menée par Raizers, première plateforme europpéenne de «crowdinvesting», offre à ses souscripteurs la possibilité d'une prise de participation au capital de Czapek. L'idée est aussi d'intégrer les actionnaires dans le processus créatif et de construction de l'entreprise, de créer ainsi un réseau social privé en incitant les actionnaires à devenir autant d'ambassadeurs de la marque – et en leur réservant des montres à prix fortement préférentiels. L'objectif est de réunir 1 million de CHF dans les mois qui viennent, afin de passer à l'industrialisation du mouvement et au lancement des premières séries de montres (objectif 1'000 montres). ■

Pour en savoir plus, allez sur http://czapek.com/investment-levels-benefits

LES VAINQUEURS DU GPHG: Prix de l'Exception Mécanique: Jaquet Droz, The Charming Bird

PUBLICITÉ

1929 Genecand Genève

Genecand traiteur sa
55 av. de la Praille | 1227 Carouge | t. 022 329 31 96 | f. 022 320 31 64 | www.genecand.ch
Honorez vos hôtes.

Figure 6.9 Report on the relaunch of Czapek, 2015.
Source: *Europa Star Switzerland*, no. 97, 2015 © Archives Europa Star.

Creating New Brands from Heritage

Hermès (see Figure 6.10). They were probably made and sold under the patronage of Jeanrenaud, a manager from Bovet Frères & Cie. This company might have used this Germanic-sounding brand name for specific markets.

As was the case for Czapek, historical research about the brand was necessary to understand its past and build a heritage strategy. However, as no archives were found in Switzerland, Guhl had to carry out brand and company research through the product itself. But, as no evidence about the history of the brand was discovered, Guhl decided to redevelop it based on technical aspects and values rather than deceased personalities. The watches he owned were from the 1930s and were mostly single-pusher split-second chronographs (*chronographe à ratrappante*). The pusher had a crenellation at the end, which allowed it to be pulled out. This is the sign of the rather rare chronographs made by Bovet Frères & Cie in Fleurier: Bovet

Figure 6.10 Chronograph Loewenthal for Hermès, undated.
Source: Personal collection. © Harry Guhl.

Figure 6.11 Pouzait wristwatch, 2024.
Source: Personal collection. © Harry Guhl.

four-stroke chronographs. The Bovet mono-rattrapante chronographs that appeared in 1936 were based on a patent by Charles Jeanrenaud. Less well known, however, is the fact that a year earlier, in 1935, Bovet, again in collaboration with Jeanrenaud, had launched a single-pusher on a classic single-pusher chronograph. There are only three beats: start, stop and reset of the chronograph hand. On the Bovet four-stroke chronograph, after the start, the user can pull back on the pusher, which stops the hand, but by pushing back on the pusher, the hand starts again without going through the reset. An intermediate time can therefore be measured in the same way as on a two-pusher chronograph.[138]

These four-stroke single-pusher chronographs are rare. They can be found mainly under Bovet and Lowenthal, the second one being a brand used by Bovet Frères & Cie during the interwar years.[139] Working together with Adrian Buchmann (Fuzion, Switzerland) and Jean-Francois Mojon (Chronode), who redesigned the Lowenthal chronograph movement with a *haute horlogerie* hand-finished appearance, Harry Guhl launched in 2024 a first collection of fifty pieces. The investment amounted to about one million francs, gathered particularly by pre-orders of half the collection.

The interest in a technical specialty of a watch movement was also the opportunity to resurrect another brand, Pouzait. Jean Moyse Pouzait (1743–93) was a watchmaker in Geneva. He has remained known as the inventor of the dead independent

Figure 6.12 Pouzait wristwatch, 2024.
Source: Personal collection. © Harry Guhl.

second, a mechanism that allows the seconds hand to be started and stopped without disturbing the movement – and therefore the measurement of the time by the watch. It has a gearing that is independent of the hour and minute hands. This system has been especially employed in watches used by doctors to determine the pulse of their patients. In the history of watchmaking, this invention by Jean Moyse Pouzait, made in 1776, is considered a major step in the development of the chronograph.[140]

Guhl observed that the deadbeat second was one of the least known yet most fascinating complications because of its pioneering mechanism and most beautiful architecture. All of the major manufactures, like Patek Philippe, Audemars Piguet, Jaeger LeCoultre and Lange & Söhne, have such a timepiece in their collections to emphasize their connection to traditional watchmaking. However, the inventor himself, Jean Moyse Pouzait, has yet to appear in any of their communication. In 2023, Guhl

Figure 6.13 Pouzait's original escapement.
Source: Personal collection. © Harry Guhl.

registered the brand and founded in early 2024 a new company in La Chaux-de-Fonds, Pouzait SA, in order to commemorate this watchmaker.[141] He commissioned historical research and developed in-house new calibres in cooperation with Adrian Buchmann (Fuzion, Switzerland). The objective is to launch deadbeat-second wristwatches as a tribute to Jean Moyse Pouzait. The relaunch of the brand cost more than three million francs. Here also, more than the personality of Pouzait itself, it was the technical specificities of his watches that inspired the development of modern products (see Figures 6.11, 6.12 and 6.13).

Conclusion

The heritage brands discussed in this chapter appear attractive to many entrepreneurs because of the image they convey. The names of the great artisan watchmakers of the past are easily associated with a wealthy clientele of aristocrats, captains of industry and other celebrities, with a few extraordinary watches in museum showcases and at auction, and with an element of mystery that sometimes surrounds their destinies. There is, however, a wide variety of cases among the new watch brands based on historical heritage. The difficulties in finding a business model that allows for sustainable growth illustrate the fact that success is not always guaranteed.

Heritage brands face two major issues. The first consists of the need to develop an excellent and unique product that appears as a tribute to the legendary name. The cases of Breguet, Czapek and Pouzait show that a modern version of special pocket watches designed in the past makes it possible to create a strong link between today's narrative and the historical legacy of the artisan. Continuity and consistency are based on technical elements. In some cases, like for most British watch masters and Daniel JeanRichard, the new wristwatches developed have little or no connection with the products developed in the past by the watchmaker being honoured. The heritage is based on vaguer elements and the brand narrative becomes weaker. Associating highly complicated watches with an old name is generally not enough to establish the legitimacy of a heritage brand. The prior existence of modernized versions of old renowned models offers this credibility, which in turn ensures greater freedom in the creation of new watch designs. However, the development of modernized versions of iconic products of the past is often costly and not profitable. Similar to Parisian haute couture, this is a necessary operation to establish the fame of a brand, but one that rarely succeeds in ensuring a company's financial equilibrium.[142]

The second issue is precisely how to build a sustainable business model to move out of the status of a niche brand and a startup company. The development of a second line – technically simpler, more affordable and positioned in accessible luxury – is one avenue for revenues and profits, like ready-to-wear and accessories for Parisian haute couture. However, the right choice of this second product is a major challenge. The example of Breguet chronograph Type XX shows that a too-low position and too-different product from the main collections can weaken the narrative and damage the brand. As for Daniel JeanRichard, it presents the case of a heritage brand that is itself the second line of another heritage brand – Girard-Perregaux. This makes it very complex to properly manage these two brands.

Graham and other niche heritage brands have chosen another way to target the increase of sales and profits outside of modernized versions of old watches: a focus on the development of modern-design highly complicated watches. The challenge is to ensure consistency between modern products and a narrative that includes historical elements that are not embodied in the product. British master watchmakers' brands emphasize well the weakness of being too focused on the product.

Conclusion

This book's analysis of brand relaunching in the watch industry, based on a large number of case studies, both successful and unsuccessful, highlights a number of points at the heart of this business model. Firstly, we have demonstrated the decisive importance of the concept as the main competitive advantage. This is what we call 'heritage', a term that expresses the reality of the concept much better than 'brand DNA', which insists on the false idea that brands naturally have a DNA and a unique character. Heritage is a concept that is socially constructed – that is, it is the result of design work that integrates distinctive elements from the brand's past with non-historical elements. As we are dealing with the awakening of sleeping beauties, the past is an important and inevitable dimension. Brands are being relaunched because managers have the idea of using elements of their history to position themselves in particular market segments or niches. As the case of Hublot demonstrates, history does not necessarily have to be very old, but a certain continuity over the decades is a necessary condition.

Historical continuity can be embodied in various elements. These include, of course, the name of a watchmaker or company, which itself conveys a long history, whether real (Breguet, Patek Philippe), imaginary (Chopard, Graham, JeanRichard) or, often, somewhere in-between (Blancpain, Czapek, Lange & Söhne, Léon Hatot). But, above all, it is the iconic products that are used to embody the permanence of a brand. The watch models developed to mark the relaunch of a brand are generally conceived as an expression of its heritage. They incorporate technical and aesthetic elements that recall the brand's past. In this respect, the relaunch of Breguet in the 1970s and 1980s is a case in point.

However, as companies often use watches with grand complications or exceptional models as the embodiment of a heritage, the question of the viability of business models often arises. These types of products have extremely high development costs, and their outlets can be relatively limited. It is therefore important to balance the business with the launch of more accessible products, which benefit from the reputation of the exceptional products and generate profits for the firm. The Calatrava and Nautilus of Patek Philippe & Cie are undoubtedly among the best successes in this respect. Their high profit margins have enabled the manufacturer to continue producing models that are more costly to develop. Many successful brands also use simplified, accessible models to ensure their profitability. Examples include Chopard's Happy Diamonds and the simpler Hublot watches. Conversely, second-line products that are too far removed from the brand's core values, such as the Breguet Type XX chronographs, can create difficulties in managing a consistent heritage. A rapid and drastic change in positioning and products, as was the case with Léon Hatot, can also lead to a profound contradiction between the brand's reconstructed heritage and the products offered to the public.

Secondly, while heritage is at the heart of brand relaunching, it also requires access to a number of resources. Capital is obviously a major resource. Reviving a sleeping beauty takes time and is expensive, especially in the early years. Brands that are part of groups such as Swatch or Richemont, or companies such as Girard Perregaux, benefit from their investments. For many independent brands, the startup model prevails. The initial investment enables the development of a few models that embody the brand's heritage. Some are then acquired by groups that give them the resources for strong growth, such as Blancpain or Lange & Söhne, while others continue to develop independently, like Graham or Czapek. Sometimes, a private equity buyout brings in a lot of fresh capital, but the pressures of short-term profitability can lead to difficulties in managing a coherent legacy. This is what happened with Breguet and Ebel after they were bought by Investcorp.

In addition to capital, technical know-how is a major resource for the revival of brands, almost all of which insist on maintaining a manufacturing tradition. Watches are generally mechanical and equipped with unique movements – the presence of a manufacture movement expressing the homage of modern managers to a brand or an old watchmaker's name. External parts and decoration are also made from special materials or using traditional methods. Access to these technical resources is an essential issue when relaunching brands. Some were quick to internalize the missing knowledge, such as Patek Philippe & Cie during the interwar years, Blancpain from the moment it was founded or when the Chaumet brothers decided to relaunch Breguet. However, direct mastery of these skills is not the only way to proceed. Several brands also use independent companies specializing in the design and production of particular movements, as well as decoration work. These include Manufacture La Joux Perret and Chronode. Until recently, Audemars

Conclusion

Piguet has played a similar role. The richness of the watchmaking ecosystem means that small companies that are close to the startup model have access to the technical resources needed to develop unique products that express the brand's heritage.

Finally, many brands work with museum curators, auction houses and historians to provide a coherent historical framework for their narrative and to reinforce their legitimacy as the embodiment of a name. While some brands distance themselves entirely from such practices and base their heritage on a relationship with a largely impressionist past (Blancpain, Graham, JeanRichard), others seek academic legitimacy for their discourse (Breguet, Czapek, Léon Hatot). Breguet is undoubtedly the best example here, since collaboration with the Musée International d'Horlogerie and collectors has been at the heart of the brand's revival strategy since the mid-1970s.

The model for awakening the sleeping beauties in the watch industry, analysed in detail in this book, which is based on building a coherent heritage and exploiting the potential offered by a vast network of independent suppliers, can be applied to other sectors of the luxury industry. The fashion and accessories business has similar characteristics in terms of industrial organization and brand management. There is, of course, a product distinction between fashion and watchmaking. In the case of the latter, the technical elements are extremely important, as they are themselves the bearers of a manufacturing tradition. They are at the heart of the heritage built up by most brands. From this perspective, fashion undoubtedly presents more difficulties in relaunching brands because it is harder to find a concrete material basis embodying continuity, apart from specific stylistic elements. However, there is a lack of studies similar to ours to be able to develop a meaningful comparison between the various luxury sectors. This book is therefore an invitation to pursue the ideas put forward here in the sectors neighbouring watchmaking.

Notes

Introduction

1. Statistics communicated by the Federation of the Swiss Watch Industry.
2. Pierre-Yves Donzé, 'La transformation de l'horlogerie suisse en industrie du luxe', in *Vers le haut de gamme made in France, Paris: Histoire économique et financière de la France*, ed. Blancheton Bertrand (Paris: IGPDE, 2021), 181–98.
3. Hervé Munz, 'Crafting time, making luxury: the heritage system and artisan revival in the Swiss watch industry, 1975–2015', in *Global Luxury: Organizational Change and Emerging Markets since the 1970s* (Singapore: Palgrave Macmillan, 2018), 197–218; Hugues Jeannerat and Olivier Crevoisier, 'Non-technological innovation and multi-local territorial knowledge dynamics in the Swiss watch industry', *International Journal of Innovation and Regional Development* 3, no. 1 (2011): 26–44.
4. *Seventh Annual Swiss Watcher*, Morgan Stanley Research, 2024.
5. For the case of Swatch Group, see Pierre-Yves Donzé, *A Business History of the Swatch Group: The Rebirth of Swiss Watchmaking and the Globalization of the Luxury Industry* (Basingstoke: Palgrave Macmillan, 2014).
6. Johanna Zanon, 'Reawakening the "sleeping beauties" of haute couture: the case of Guy and Arnaud de Lummen', in *European Fashion: The Creation of a Global Industry*, ed. Regina Lee Blaszczyk and Véronique Pouillard (Manchester: Manchester University Press, 2020), 86–116.

Chapter 1

1. Cambridge Dictionary, accessed 13 October 2023, https://dictionary.cambridge.org/.
2. Jean-Noël Kapferer and Vincent Bastien, *The Luxury Strategy: Break the Rules of Marketing to Build Luxury Brands* (New York: Kogan Page Publishers, 2012).
3. Sophie Boutillier and Dimitri Uzunidis, 'Entrepreneurs historiques de l'industrie du luxe et innovation permanente', *Innovations* 2 (2013): 91–115.
4. Christopher M. Moore and Grete Birtwistle, 'The nature of parenting advantage in luxury fashion retailing – the case of Gucci group NV,' *International Journal of Retail & Distribution Management* 33, no. 4 (2005): 256–70; Mark Tungate, *Luxury World: The Past, Present and Future of Luxury Brands* (New York: Kogan Page Publishers, 2009).
5. Pierre-Yves Donzé, *Selling Europe to the World: The Rise of the Luxury Fashion Industry, 1980–2020* (London: Bloomsbury, 2023), chapters 1–3.

Notes

6. Pierre-Yves Donzé and Ben Wubs, 'Storytelling and the making of a global luxury fashion brand: Christian Dior', *International Journal of Fashion Studies* 6, no. 1 (2019): 83–102.
7. Johanna Zanon, 'Reawakening the "sleeping beauties" of haute couture: the case of Guy and Arnaud de Lummen', in *European Fashion* (Manchester: Manchester University Press, 2020), 86–116.
8. Florence Brachet Champsaur, 'Madeleine Vionnet and Galeries Lafayette: the unlikely marriage of a Parisian couture house and a French department store, 1922–40', *Business History* 54, no. 1 (2012): 48–66.
9. Zanon, 'Reawakening the "sleeping beauties" of haute couture', 100.
10. Zanon, ibid. 96.
11. *Les Echos*, 23 May 2012.
12. Fashion Network, 16 October 2018, https://fr.fashionnetwork.com/ (accessed 13 October 2023).
13. *Nikkei Asia*, 15 December 2020.
14. *Nikkei Asia*, 4 March 2020.
15. Trinity, Annual Report, 2019.
16. *Nikkei Asia*, 14 December 2020.
17. Delphine Dion, 'How to manage heritage brands: The Case of Sleeping Beauties Revival', in *Oxford Handbook of Luxury Business*, ed. Pierre-Yves Donzé, Véronique Pouillard and Joanne Roberts (New York: Oxford University Press, 2022), 279–80.
18. Donzé, *Selling Europe to the World*, 88–89.
19. 'Investcorp SA', *International Directory of Company Histories* (Gale, 2004, vol. 57), 179–82.
20. Ibid., 179.
21. Zanon, 104–5.
22. Database of the Institut National de la Propriété Intellectueelle (INPI), https://data.inpi.fr/ (accessed 13 October 2023).
23. *Les Echos*, 16 March 2012.
24. *New York Times*, 20 October 2014 and 5 July 2017.
25. Dephine Dion and Gérald Mazzalovo, 'Reviving sleeping beauty brands by rearticulating brand heritage', *Journal of Business Research* 69, no. 12 (2016): 5894–900.
26. Dion and Mazzalovo, ibid.; https://www.lacoste.com (accessed 15 October 2023).
27. *Financial Times*, 23 February 1983 and 8 February 1990.
28. *Les Echos*, 25 January 2013.
29. *Fashion Network*, 18 September 2018.
30. Delphine Dion, 'How to manage heritage brands: The Case of Sleeping Beauties Revival', in *Oxford Handbook of Luxury Business*, ed. Pierre-Yves Donzé, Véronique Pouillard and Joanne Roberts (New York: Oxford University Press, 2022), 278.
31. François-Marie Grau, *La haute couture* (Paris: PUF, 2000), 24.
32. Official website of Elsa Schiaparelli, https://www.schiaparelli.com (accessed 15 October 2023).

33. Mats Urde, Stephen A. Greyser and John M. T. Balmer, 'Corporate brands with a heritage', *Journal of Brand Management* 15 (2007): 4–5.
34. Ibid., 5.
35. Ibid., 9–11.
36. Valerie Steele, *Paris Fashion: A Cultural History* (Oxford and New York: Oxford University Press, 1988); Didier Grumbach, *History of International Fashion* (Northampton: Interlink Books, 2014).
37. Chantal Trubert-Tollu, Françoise Tétart-Vittu, Jean-Marie Martin-Hattemberg and Fabrice Olivieri, *The House of Worth, 1858–1954: The Birth of Haute Couture* (London: Thames & Hudson, 2017).
38. On Cartier, see Francesca Cartier Brickell, *Cartier: The Untold Story of the Family Behind the Jewelry Empire* (New York: Ballantine Books, 2019).
39. Grau, *La haute couture*, 24. In 1999, there were only sixteen haute couture houses in Paris.
40. Pouillard, Véronique, *Paris to New York: The Transatlantic Fashion Industry in the Twentieth Century* (Cambridge, MA: Harvard University Press, 2021); Pierre-Yves Donzé and Ben Wubs, 'Storytelling and the making of a global luxury fashion brand: Christian Dior', *International Journal of Fashion Studies* 6, no. 1 (2019): 83–102.
41. Rhonda Garelick, 'Lagerfeld, Fashion, and Cultural Heritage', *English Language Notes* 60, no. 2 (2022): 156–74.
42. Donzé and Wubs, 'Storytelling and the making of a global luxury fashion brand'.
43. Zanon, ibid., 87.
44. Delphine Dion, 'How to manage heritage brands: The Case of Sleeping Beauties Revival', in *Oxford Handbook of Luxury Business*, ed. Pierre-Yves Donzé, Véronique Pouillard and Joanne Roberts (New York: Oxford University Press, 2022), 273–86.
45. Juliana Luna Mora and Jess Berry, 'Creative direction succession in luxury fashion: The illusion of immortality at Chanel and Alexander McQueen', *Luxury* 9, no. 2–3 (2022): 117–40.
46. Marrou Henri-Irénée, *De la connaissance historique* (Paris: Seuil, 1954).
47. Edward H. Carr, *What is History?* (Cambridge: Cambridge University Press, 1961).
48. Michael J. Hogan (ed.), *Hiroshima in History and Memory* (Cambridge: Cambridge University Press, 1996).
49. Eric Hobsbawm and T. Ranger (eds.), *The Invention of Tradition* (Cambridge: Cambridge University Press, 1983).
50. Chanel official website, https://www.chanel.com/us/about-chanel/the-founder/ (accessed 19 October 2023). On Chanel, see also Geoffrey Jones and Emily Grandjean, *Coco Chanel: From Fashion Icon to Nazi Agent*, Harvard Business School, case no. 9-318-139, 2023.
51. Delphine Dion and Gérald Mazzalovo, 'Reviving sleeping beauty brands by rearticulating brand heritage', *Journal of Business Research* 69, no. 12 (2016): 5894–900.

Notes

52. Dion, ibid., 275.
53. Cartier official website, https://www.cartier.com/en-us/la-maison/the-story/lodyssee-de-cartier/ (accessed 19 October 2023).

Chapter 2

1. Pierre-Yves Donzé, *Selling Europe to the World*: *The Rise of the Luxury Fashion Industry, 1980–2020* (London: Bloomsbury Publishing, 2023), chapters 1–3.
2. Pierre-Yves Donzé, *The Business of Time: A Global History of the Watch Industry* (Manchester: Manchester University Press, 2022).
3. Pierre-Yves Donzé, *L'invention du luxe: histoire de l'horlogerie à Genève de 1815 à nos jours* (Neuchâtel, Alphil, 2017); Hugues Jeannerat and Olivier Crevoisier, 'Non-technological innovation and multi-local territorial knowledge dynamics in the Swiss watch industry', *International Journal of Innovation and Regional Development* 3, no. 1 (2011): 26–44; Laurence Marti, *Le renouveau horloger: Contribution à une histoire récente de l'horlogerie suisse (1980–2015)* (Neuchâtel: Alphil, 2016); Hervé Munz, *La transmission en jeu: Apprendre, pratiquer, patrimonialiser l'horlogerie en Suisse* (Neuchâtel: Alphil, 2016); Ryan Raffaelli, 'Technology reemergence: Creating new value for old technologies in Swiss mechanical watchmaking, 1970–2008', *Administrative Science Quarterly* 64, no. 3 (2019): 576–618; Kayhan Tajeddini and Myfanwy Trueman, 'The potential for innovativeness: a tale of the Swiss watch industry', *Journal of Marketing Management* 24, no. 1–2 (2008): 169–84.
4. Nicholas Foulkes, *Patek Philippe: The Authorized Biography* (London: Preface Publishing, 2017).
5. Statistics communicated to the author by Patek Philippe.
6. Estelle Fallet, 'Piaget', *Dictionnaire historique de la Suisse*, www.dhs.ch (accessed 23 June 2024).
7. Donzé, *L'invention du luxe*, 126.
8. Pierre-Yves Donzé, 'Industrial leadership and the long-lasting competitiveness of the Swiss watch industry', in Martin Guttmann (ed.), *Historians on Leadership and Strategy: Case Studies From Antiquity to Modernity* (Cham: Springer, 2020), 171–91.
9. Marco Richon, *Omega Saga* (Bienne: Fondation Brandt, 1998).
10. *Le Nouveau Quotidien*, 5 August 1992, *The Swatch Group* (Geneva: Helvea, 2007), p. 21.
11. Pierre-Yves Donzé, *A business history of the Swatch Group: The Rebirth of Swiss Watchmaking and the Globalization of the Luxury Industry* (Basingstoke: Palgrave Macmillan, 2014), 72–5.
12. Ibid., 117–18.
13. Press release of Richemont, 2 July 2024, https://www.richemont.com/news-media/press-releases-news/richemont-appoints-louis-ferla-as-ceo-of-cartier/ (accessed 25 October 2024).

14. Donzé, *A Business History of the Swatch Group*, 119–20.
15. Ibid., 116–17.
16. *Le Temps*, 22 September 2010.
17. Pierre-Yves Donzé, *The Making of a Status Symbol: a Business History of Rolex* (Manchester: Manchester University Press, 2025).
18. Euromonitor International, Passport Database, https://login.euromonitor.com (accessed 10 November 2024).
19. COSC, Annual Report, 2000 and Morgan Stanley, Report on Swiss Luxury Watches, 2024.
20. Pierre-Yves Donzé, *History of the Swiss Watch Industry from Jacques David to Nicholas Hayek* (Berne: Peter Lang, 2015), 141; and Morgan Stanley, Report on Swiss Luxury Watches, 2024.
21. *Europa Star Europe*, 2000, no. 242, pp. 12–18.
22. *Le Temps*, 29 December 2023.
23. Swatch Group, Annual Report, 2008–23.
24. https://www.counterpointresearch.com/insights/global-smartwatch-shipments-market-share/ (accessed 10 November 2024).
25. *Vontobel Luxury Goods Shop* (Zurich: Vontobel, 2018); Strategy Analytics, https://news.strategyanalytics.com/press-release/devices/strategy-analytics-apple-watch-captures-half-18-million-global-smartwatch (accessed 29 August 2019).
26. *Le Temps* (26 May 2016 and 14 March 2017).
27. Pierre-Yves Donzé, David Borel and Jean-Baptiste Porier, 'L'innovation dans les montres connectées: une analyse des dépôts de brevets, 2010-2020', *Bulletin de la Société suisse de chronométrie* 92 (2022): 37–42.
28. Donzé, *L'invention du luxe*, 174–80.
29. http://www.gphg.org/horlogerie/fr/fondation (accessed 23 September 2015).
30. Donzé, *L'invention du luxe*, 178–80.

Chapter 3

1. On this transformation, see Donzé, 'La transformation de l'horlogerie suisse en industrie du luxe'.
2. K. Moore and S. Reid, 'The birth of brand: 4000 years of branding', *Business History* 50, no. 4 (2008): 419–32.
3. Ibid.
4. Teresa da Silva Lopes, Bruna Dourado and Elizabeth Santos de Souza, 'Unbundling the brand: Differentiation and the law in the Brazilian South American tea industry', *Business History* 66, no. 4 (2022): 1–24; Patricio Sáiz and Rafael Castro (eds), *The Brand and Its History: Trademarks, Branding and National Identity* (London: Routledge, 2022).

5. MIH, *Archives de l'horlogerie* (volume 1, 1892), 3.
6. P. Sáiz and R. Castro, 'Trademarks in branding: Legal issues and commercial practices', *Business History* 60, no. 8 (2018): 1105–26.
7. Alfred Chandler, *Scale and Scope Scale and Scope: The Dynamics of Industrial Capitalism* (Cambridge, MA: Harvard University Press, 1990), 63–5 and 168–70.
8. Geoffrey Jones, *Multinationals and Global Capitalism: From the Nineteenth to the Twenty First Century* (New York: Oxford University Press, 2005), 87.
9. Geoffrey Jones, *Beauty Imagined: A History of the Global Beauty Industry* (New York: Oxford University Press, 2010), 130.
10. Stefan Schwarzkopf, 'Turning trademarks into brands: How advertising agencies practiced and conceptualized branding, 1890–1930', in *Trademarks, Brands, and Competitiveness* (London and New York: Routledge, 2010), 168, 187–215.
11. Nicolas Chachereau, *Les débuts du système suisse des brevets d'invention (1873–1914)* (Neuchâtel: Alphil, 2022), 83–5.
12. MIH, *Archives de l'horlogerie* (volume 1, 1892), 4.
13. Ibid.
14. Patrick Linder, *Longines, un sablier et des ailes : histoire, enjeux, construction d'une marque: 120 ans de la protection d'un logotype (1889–2009)* (Saint-Imier: Longines, 2009); Pierre-Yves Donzé, *La fabrique de l'excellence: histoire de Rolex* (Neuchâtel: Alphil, 2024).
15. Linder, *Histoire, enjeux, construction d'une marque*, 33; J. Borloz, *100 ans Office fédéral de la Propriété Intellectuelle* (Bern: Bundesamt für Geistiges Eigentum, 1988).
16. Pierre-Yves Donzé, 'The transformation of global luxury brands: The case of the Swiss watch company Longines, 1880–2010', *Business History* 62, no. 1 (2020): 26–41.
17. David M. Higgins, *Brands, Geographical Origin, and the Global Economy: A History from the Nineteenth Century to the Present* (Cambridge: Cambridge University Press, 2018).
18. Pierre-Yves Donzé, 'National labels and the competitiveness of European industries: the example of the "Swiss Made" law since 1950', *European Review of History* 26, no. 5 (2019): 855–70.
19. *L'Impartial*, 8 June 1890 and 15 May 1891.
20. *L'Impartial*, 24 June 1892, 18 November 1892 and 18 June 1894.
21. Swiss official trade statistics published in the *Journal suisse d'horlogerie*, 1890–1894.
22. Jones, *Multinationals and Global Capitalism*, 197–8.
23. Theodore Levitt, 'The globalization of markets', *Harvard Business Review* 61 (1983): 3.
24. Jean-Noël Kapferer, 'The post-global brand', *Journal of Brand Management* 12, no. 5 (2005): 319–24.
25. Jones, *Beauty Imagined*, 360.
26. Jones, *Beauty Imagined*, 361.
27. Da Silva Lopes, *Global Brands*.
28. Richon, *Omega Saga*, chapter 4.

29. Pierre-Yves Donzé, *The Making of a Status Symbol*, chapter 5.
30. Donzé, 'The transformation of global luxury brands'.
31. Archives Longines (AL), B32.5, minutes of the Board meeting, 30 November 1956.
32. Ibid.
33. Ibid.
34. Ibid.
35. Ibid.
36. MIH, Archives de l'horlogerie, 1950–59.
37. AL, annual report of the technical manager, 1946–57.
38. AL, B32.5, Board minutes, 11 September 1975.
39. *Seiko*, 291–3.
40. Pierre-Yves Donzé, *The Business of Time: Global History of the Watch Industry* (Manchester: Manchester University Press, 2022).
41. Blanc Jean-François, *Suisse-Hong Kong, le défi horloger …*, 144–5.
42. *Journal de Genève*, 18 November 1958; E. Martin-Achard, 'La Nationalité Suisse De La Montre', *La semaine judiciaire* 81, no. 10 (1959): 145–67.
43. Rapport de la Commission pour l'étude des prix, *Etude critique des conditions de concurrence dans l'industrie horlogère suisse*, March 1959. I address my best thanks to Sabine Pitteloud for having given me this reference.
44. Between 1972 and 1979, only 0.3 per cent of Swiss watches exported were controlled. Donzé, *History of the Swiss Watch Industry*, 122.
45. Letter from the Swiss consulate in Hong Kong to the Division of Trade of the Federal Department of Public Economy, 17 November 1967. Swiss Diplomatic Documents Database (Dodis), https://dodis.ch/32554 (accessed 5 June 2024).
46. Jean-Daniel Pasche, *La protection des armoiries fédérales et de l'indication 'suisse'* (Neuchâtel: Editions Ides et Calendes, 1988), 88–90.
47. Donzé, *The Business of Time*, chapter 7.
48. Donzé, *A Business History of the Swatch Group: The Rebirth of Swiss Watchmaking and the Globalization of the Luxury Industry* (Basingstoke: Palgrave Macmillan, 2014).
49. Teresa Lopes, *Global Brands*; Donzé Pierre-Yves, *Selling Europe to the World: the Rise of the Luxury Fashion Industry, 1980–2020* (London: Bloomsbury, 2023).
50. Pierre-Yves Donzé, 'The transformation of global luxury brands: The case of the Swiss watch company Longines, 1880–2010', *Business History* 62, no. 1 (2020): 26–41.
51. D. Allères, 'Spécificités et stratégies marketing des différents univers du luxe', *Revue française du marketing* 8 (1991): 115–46.
52. Henry Bédat Jacqueline, *Une région, une passion: l'horlogerie. Une entreprise: Longines*. Compagnie des Montres Longines Francillon, 1992.
53. Trueb, *World of Watches*, 424.

Chapter 4

1. Pierre-Yves Donzé, *Industrial Development, Technology Transfer, and Global Competition: The Japanese watch industry from 1850 to the present day* (New York: Routledge, 2017).
2. *L'Impartial*, 27 April 1981.
3. Donzé, *La fabrique de l'excellence*, chapter 7.
4. Morgan Stanley Research, 2023.
5. *Europa Star*, no. 134, 2023, 20–1.
6. Pierre-Yves Donzé and Ben Wubs, 'LVMH: Storytelling and organizing creativity in luxury and fashion', *European Fashion* (Manchester: Manchester University Press, 2020), 63–85.
7. *Europa Star*, no. 134, 2023, 18; Dictionnaire du Jura, www.diju.ch (accessed 10 September 2023); and *Feuille officielle Suisse du commerce (FOSC)*, 14 December 1998.
8. Donzé, *The Business of Time*, chapter 7.
9. For the example of Raketa, see *Europa Star*, no. 357, 2020, page 62. For Chronotechna, see Král, Petr, 'Could there be a luxury brand originating from the Czech Republic? The case of the Czech watchmaker Prim', *Central European Business Review* 2, no. 3 (2013): 15–21.
10. Pierre-Yves Donzé, 'Global competition and technological innovation: a new interpretation of the watch crisis, 1970s–1980s', in David Thomas, Jon Mathieu, Janick Marina Schaufelbuehl and Tobias Straumann (eds), *Crises – Causes, Interpretations and Consequences* (Zurich: Chronos, 2012), 275–89.
11. Donzé, *A Business History of the Swatch Group*.
12. Hervé Munz, *La transmission en jeu: apprendre, pratiquer, patrimonialiser: l'horlogerie en Suisse* (Neuchâtel: Alphil, 2016).
13. Ibid., 132–3.
14. WIPO Global Brand Database, https://www.wipo.int/reference/en/branddb/, accessed 3 June 2024; *FOSC*, 27 November 1989.
15. Donzé, *L'invention du luxe*, 136–8.
16. Blancpain Claude, *La famille Blancpain*, Nonan-sur-Matran Fribourg: C. Blancpain, 1994, 103.
17. Richon Marco, *Omega Saga* (Biel: Fondation Brandt, 1998).
18. *Journal de Genève*, 6 July 1961.
19. *FOSC*, 28 July 1980.
20. *FOSC*, 25 May 1982 and Helvea, 2006, 13.
21. *Journal de Genève*, 12 June 1987.
22. *FOSC*, 12 December 1983.
23. *FOSC*, 22 February 1984.
24. *Gazette de Lausanne*, 4 April 1987; *FOSC*, 20 November 1978.

25. *Gazette de Lausanne*, 4 April 1987.
26. *FOSC*, 22 September 1980.
27. *FOSC*, 2 March 1982, 7 July 1982, 22 November 1983. The textile company was Textiles Berger SA, in Eclepens.
28. Blancpain, *La famille Blancpain*, op. cit., 89. The historical development of the firm summarised here is based on this source (pp. 89–102), as well as Laurence Marti, *Une région au rythme du temps: Histoire socio-économique du Vallon de Saint-Imier, 1700–2007* (Saint-Imier: Edition des Longines, 2007).
29. *FOSC*, 17 August 1933.
30. *Le Nouveau Quotidien*, 13 October 1991.
31. Bernard Prongué (ed.), *L'écartèlement: espace jurassien et identité plurielle* (Saint-Imier: Canevas, 1991).
32. *Journal de Genève*, 12 June 1987.
33. *Journal de Genève*, 12 June 1987 and 9 July 1992.
34. Donzé, *Selling Europe to the World*, chapter 2.
35. *Le Nouveau Quotidien*, 8 July 1992.
36. Ibid.
37. Donzé, *A Business History of the Swatch Group*.
38. *Europa Star Asia*, no. 261, 1994, 38–9; *Europa Star Europe*, no. 221, 1997, 44; *Journal de Genève*, 28 April 1997.
39. *FOSC*, 10 July 2003 and 12 February 2004. It is also important to note that the name of Biver has been nearly completely erased from the official history of Blancpain. See the website of the brand, https://www.blancpain.com/en/brand/our-vision/history, accessed 8 September 2023.
40. Swatch Group, Annual Report, 2002 and 2005.
41. Donzé, *A Business History of Swatch Group*, 82–3.
42. *Europa Star*, no. 103, 2017, 28–9.
43. Helvea, Vontobel Equity Research and Morgan Stanley.
44. Morgan Stanley.
45. *A Business History of the Swatch Group*.
46. Ibid., 73.
47. *Fine Jewels and Watches from the Atelier of Leon Hatot* (Geneva: Christie's, 1989).
48. WIPO, Global Brand Database, https://branddb.wipo.int, accessed 4 September 2023.
49. Biver is mentioned as the member of Swatch Group's executive committee in charge of Léon Hatot in 2000. Swatch Group, Annual Report, 2000.
50. Claude Briselance, *Les écoles d'horlogerie de Besançon: une contribution décisive au développement industriel local et régional (1793–1974)* (Université de Lyon II, thèse de doctorat non publiée, 2015, vol. 1), 549–50.
51. *Montres Passion*, no. 30, 2007, 86.
52. Michel Viredaz, 'Léon Hatot et les horloges électriques ATO', *Chronométrophilia* 56 (2004): 67–77 (here 68).

53. *Montres Passion*, no. 30, 2007, 86.
54. Espacenet, Database of the European Patent Office, https://worldwide.espacenet.com/patent/ (accessed 4 September 2023).
55. *Montres Passion*, no. 30, 2007, 86.
56. *FOSC*, 29 November 2001.
57. Swatch Group, Annual Report, 2004, 101.
58. *Europa Star*, no. 267, 2004, 20.
59. Swatch Group, Annual Report, 2004, 33.
60. *Europa Star*, no. 267, 2004, 22.
61. *Europa Star*, no. 267, 2004, 22.
62. *Montres Passion*, no. 30, 2007, 86.
63. *Europa Star*, no. 267, 2004, 22.
64. Arlette-Elsa Emch, *Léon Hatot* (Paris: Assouline, 2005).
65. Swatch Group, Annual Report, 2005, 38.
66. Swatch Group, Annual Report, 2003–7.
67. *FOSC*, 26 January 2006.
68. Helvea, *The Swatch Group*, 30 March 2007.
69. Vontobel Equity Research.
70. *Montres Passion*, no. 30, 2007, 86.
71. Swatch Group, Annual Report, 2009, 51.
72. Ibidem.
73. *Le Temps*, 14 October 2009.
74. *FOSC*, 29 May 2009, 24 December 2009 and 22 July 2010.
75. *Le Temps*, 20 June 2012.
76. Donzé, *A Business History of the Swatch Group*, 75.
77. *Le Temps*, 14 January 2013.
78. *FOSC*, 24 June 2013.
79. *FOSC*, 10 June 2014.
80. *Le Temps*, 14 October 2009.
81. Swatch Group, Annual Report, 2008–10.
82. Vontobel Equity Research.
83. The top ten largest jewellery brands had a total market share of only 12.8 per cent in 2018, while it was 73.5 per cent for watch brands. Donzé, *Selling Europe to the World*, 113.
84. Pierre-Yves Donzé, *L'invention du luxe: histoire de l'horlogerie à Genève de 1815 à nos jours* (Neuchâtel: Alphil, 2017), 133.
85. On the German watch industry, see Hans-Heinrich Schmid, *Lexikon der Deutschen Uhrenindustrie 1850–1980* (Nuremberg: German Society for Chronometrie, vol. 2, 2017).
86. Gustav Speckhart, *Peter Henlein der Erfinder der Taschenuhr: fachgeschichtliche Abhandlung* (Nuremberg: Verl. J.L., 1890).
87. Schmid, *Lexikon der Deutschen Uhrenindustrie*, vol. 2, 386–7.

88. Ibid.
89. Ibid., 190.
90. *L'Impartial*, 25 August 1967.
91. Schmid, *Lexicon of the German Watch Industry*, 318.
92. Egana Goldpfeil, Annual Report 2000.
93. WIPO, Global Brand Database, https://branddb.wipo.int (accessed 9 September 2023).
94. *FOSC*, 21 August 1991.
95. David Seyffer, *Die Unternehmensgeschichte von IWC Schaffhausen: Ein Schweizer Uhrenhersteller zwischen Innovation und Tradition*, Oberhausen: Athena Verlag, 2014, 218–19.
96. Donzé, *L'invention du luxe*, 160–1.
97. Archives Swisstime, September 2002.
98. *FOSC*, 18 April 1986.
99. Archives Swisstime, March 2006.
100. Vontobel Equity Research, 2013 and Morgan Stanley Research, 2023.
101. Morgan Stanley Research, 2023.
102. *Europa Star*, no. 214, 1995, 125–6.
103. Schmid, *Lexicon of the German Watch Industry*, 186 and 190.
104. Ibid.
105. Archives Swisstime, October 2011 and *Europa Star*, no. 110, 2018, 22.
106. Swatch Group, Annual Report, 2001–4.
107. Helvea, *The Swatch Group*, 2006, 13–14.
108. Helvea, *The Swatch Group*, 2006, 21.
109. Vontobel Equity Research, 2011 and 2016.
110. Morgan Stanley Research, 2020 and 2023.
111. Morgan Stanley Research, 2023. The average price was slightly higher in the 2010s according to Vontobel Equity Research.
112. Swatch Group, Annual Report, 2008, 10 and 62.
113. Vontobel Equity Research, 2011 and 2018.
114. Morgan Stanley Research, 2022.

Chapter 5

1. Francesca Cartier Brickell, *The Cartiers: The Untold Story of the Family Behind the Jewelry Empire* (New York: Ballantine Books, 2019); Donzé, *Selling Europe to the World*, 43–45.
2. *FOSC*, 27 July 1979.
3. *FOSC*, 26 January 1980.
4. *Journal du Jura*, 25 November 1994.

5. Vontobel Equity Research, 2011.
6. *Le Temps*, 28 April 2017.
7. *Europa Star*, Swiss Edition, 2023, no. 134, 28–9.
8. Pierre-Yves Donzé, *The Business of Time*, 125.
9. http://www.stelux.com/eng/ir/profile.php, accessed 29 September 2023.
10. *Le Temps*, 16 December 2023.
11. Nicholas Foulkes, *Patek Philippe: le biographie autorisée* (London: Preface, 2016).
12. Foulkes, *Patek Philippe*, 60.
13. *FOSC*, 1901, 286–7.
14. Foulkes, 115.
15. Foulkes, 122–7.
16. Espacenet Database, https://worldwide.espacenet.com/ (accessed 30 September 2023).
17. Foulkes, 150; *Statistiques historiques de la Suisse*, 627.
18. Foulkes, 154.
19. *Journal de Genève*, 12 April 1931.
20. Ibid.
21. An article in *Journal de Genève* published in 1926 explained the advantage of this company against industrial factories during the period of crisis. *Journal de Genève*, 25 March 1926.
22. Pierre-Yves Donzé, *History of the Swiss Watch Industry from Jacques David to Nicolas Hayek* (Berne: Peter Lang, third edition, 2011), 92.
23. *Journal de Genève*, 26 March 1933.
24. *FOSC*, 24 June 1931.
25. *FOSC*, 22 June 1933.
26. *FOSC*, 22 June 1933; Foulkes, 165.
27. *FOSC*, 13 August 1935.
28. On Tavannes Watch, see Christine Gagnebin-Diacon, *La fabrique et le village: la Tavannes Watch Co. (1890–1918)* (Porrentruy: CEH, 1996).
29. Foulkes, 166–7.
30. Foulkes, 173.
31. *Journal de Genève*, 16 August 1937.
32. *Patek Philippe 175* (Geneva: Christie's, 2014), 133 and 219.
33. Espacenet. The years are the years of first publication.
34. Sotheby's official website, https://www.sothebys.com/en/articles/ref-2499-an-unparalleled-wristwatch-by-patek-philippe (accessed 2 October 2023).
35. *Patek Philippe 175* (Geneva: Christie's, 2014), 18.
36. Ibid., 15.
37. *Journal de Genève*, 16 April 1945.
38. Foulkes, 186.
39. Foulkes, 196.

40. Robin Moschard et Emma Chatelain, 'Chopard, Genève', *Dictionnaire du Jura (DIJU)*, https://diju.ch/f/notices/detail/1000216-chopard-geneve (accessed 18 September 2023).
41. *FOSC*, 1883, 123.
42. *FOSC*, 1884, page 26 and 1885, page 602.
43. *FOSC*, 1904–9.
44. Patents CH65947 and CH67934. Espacenet, https://worldwide.espacenet.com/patent/ (accessed 18 September 2023).
45. *FOSC*, June 20,1922.
46. *FOSC*, 16 September 1936.
47. Donzé, *L'invention du luxe*, 89–91.
48. Archives Europa Star, *Trade Bulletin*, no. 209, 1950, 6.
49. Karl-Friedrich Scheufele, 'Postface', in *Family Business: Key Issues*, ed. Denise Kenyon-Rouvinez and John L. Ward (Basingstoke: Palgrave Macmillan, 2005), 77.
50. *FOSC*, 3 November 1964.
51. Iris Wimmer-Olbort, *1904–2004: Karl Scheufele: une entreprise familiale au fil du temps*, 2004.
52. *FOSC*, 2 October 1970. The address of this company, whose president was Geor Lauer, was the headquarters of Chopard.
53. *Journal de Genève*, 12 April 1975.
54. *Europa Star*, no. 100, 1976, 75.
55. *Montres Passion*, vol. 1, 1993, 49.
56. *FOSC*, 13 May 1994.
57. Archives Europa Star, *Trade Bulletin*, no. 1091, 1997, 6.
58. Ibid.
59. *FOSC*, 30 January 1996.
60. *FOSC*, 14 July 2008.
61. Donzé, *A Business History of Swatch Group*, 126–9.
62. *FOSC*, 1 December 2009. The address of Chronomètres Ferdinand Berthoud SA is the same as Chopard Manufacture SA.
63. *Europa Star*, no. 135, 2023, 16.
64. Ibid.
65. Ibid.
66. Its market share fluctuated between 1.6 per cent and 1.4 per cent during these years. Its rank as a luxury jewellery brand was, however, only eighth, as some companies (LVMH and Richemont) own more than one competitive brand. Euromonitor, Passport, Luxury Jewelry, accessed 19 September 2023.
67. JETRO, *Suisu no kinzokusei tokei bando shijo chosa* (Osaka: JETRO, 1982).
68. Morgan Stanley, 2023.
69. Donzé, *A Business History of the Swatch Group*, 133.
70. *L'Impartial*, 9 January 2004.
71. *L'Impartial*, 14 June 2004.

Notes

72. *Europa Star*, no. 176, 1989, 132.
73. *FOSC*, 8 June 1978, 22 March 1980 and 2 July 1980.
74. *FOSC*, 18 February 1980 and 20 January 1981.
75. *Europa Star*, no. 120, 1980, 268.
76. *Europa Star*, no. 177, 1980, 80.
77. *FOSC*, 6 July 1982 and 18 March 1983.
78. Pierre-Yves Donzé, *La fabrique de l'excellence: Histoire de Rolex* (Neuchâtel: Alphil, 2024).
79. *FOSC*, 21 February 1986.
80. *FOSC*, 11 January 1990.
81. *Europa Star*, Asia Edition, 1988, no. 224, 68.
82. *Europa Star*, Asia Edition, 1988, no. 224, 68.
83. Ibid.
84. *FOSC*, 17 March 1982. This company was dissolved in 1997. *FOSC*, 12 December 1997.
85. *Europa Star*, no. 176, 1989, 132.
86. *Europa Star*, Europe Edition, 1993, no. 198, 380; *Europa Star*, Europe Edition, 1993, no. 199, 120.
87. *Europa Star*, 1994–2003.
88. On responsible values, see Geoffrey Jones, *Deeply Responsible Business: A Global History of Values-Driven Leadership* (Cambridge, MA: Harvard University Press, 2023).
89. *Europa Star*, Europe Edition, 1998, no. 229, 24.
90. *Europa Star*, Europe Edition, 1999, no. 232, 88.
91. *Europa Star*, Europe Edition, 1997, no. 217, 64; *Europa Star*, Europe Edition, 2004, no. 286, 24.
92. Pierre-Yves Donzé, 'Industrial leadership and the long-lasting competitiveness of the Swiss watch industry,' in Guttmann Martin (ed.), *Historians on Leadership and Strategy: Case Studies from Antiquity to Modernity* (Cham: Springer, 2020), 171–91.
93. *FOSC*, 6 July 2004, 30 July 2004, 4 November 2004 and 16 December 2004.
94. WOPI brand database, https://www.wipo.int/reference/en/branddb/, and Espacenet, global patent database, https://worldwide.espacenet.com (accessed 25 September 2023).
95. *Europa Star*, Europe Edition, 2004, no. 286, 25.
96. Ibid., 26.
97. *Europa Star*, Europe Edition, 2005, no. 271, 31.
98. https://www.hublot.com/fr-is/craftsmanship/innovative-materials (accessed 25 May 2021).
99. Ibid., 25.
100. See the official website of the brand, https://www.hublot.com/en-ch/our-world, accessed 25 September 2023.
101. *Le Temps*, 25 April 2008.
102. Morgan Stanley, 2023.

103. *Europa Star*, Europe Edition, 1963, no. 22, 60–6.
104. Estelle Fallet: 'Corum', in *Dictionnaire historique de la Suisse (DHS)*, version du 09.07.2019, https://hls-dhs-dss.ch/fr/articles/046456/2019-07-09/ (accessed 27 September 2023); *FOSC*, 14 March 1924.
105. *FOSC*, 24 June 1956.
106. *Europa Star*, Europe Edition, 1980, no. 124, 32.
107. *Europa Star*, Europe Edition, 1990, no, 183, 54.
108. *L'Impartial*, 23 October 1998.
109. *Europa Star*, Europe Edition, 1999, no. 232, 74.
110. *Europa Star*, Europe Edition, 1999, no. 234, 90–1.
111. *Los Angeles Times*, 26 March 1995; Pierre-Yves Donzé, 'Fashion watches: The emergence of accessory makers as intermediaries in the fashion system', *International Journal of Fashion Studies* 4, no. 1 (2017): 73–4.
112. *FOSC*, 4 May 2000.
113. *Europa Star*, Europe Edition, 2002, no. 252, 116–18.
114. *Europa Star*, Europe Edition, 1999, no. 232, 74; Vontobel Equity Research, 2011.
115. *L'Impartial*, 10 January 2008.
116. *Le Temps*, 21 May 2017.
117. Citychamps, Annual Reports, 2005–22.
118. Ibid.
119. *Le Temps*, 18 August 2014 and 21 February 2016.
120. Vontobel Equity Research, 2011; Morgan Stanley, 2018.
121. *FOSC*, 22 July 1911.
122. *FOSC*, 1 September 1970.
123. *L'Hebdo*, 24 November 2011.
124. Pierre-Yves Donzé, *Selling Europe to the World*, 43–5.
125. Hamida Aman, *L'évolution de la communication publicitaire: le cas de l'entreprise Ebel de 1911 à 2001* (University of Lausanne, unpublished Master's thesis, 2002), 18.
126. Ibid., 19.
127. Ibid., 20.
128. *FOSC*, 29 May 1987 and 14 June 1988.
129. Aman, 22.
130. *Europa Star*, Europe Edition, 1994, no. 207, 34; *L'Impartial*, 5 September 1996.
131. *L'Impartial*, 5 September 1996.
132. *Europa Star*, Europe Edition, 1995, no. 214, 38–9. Ebel kept 'The Architects of Time' as a slogan, but the communication concept was completely renewed.
133. Donzé, *Selling Europe to the World*, 65.
134. LVMH, Annual report, 2002–3.
135. *Europa Star*, Swiss Edition, 2006, no. 43, 7.
136. Movado Group, Annual report (Form 10-K), 2005.
137. *Europa Star*, Swiss Edition, 2006, no. 43, 7.
138. *Europa Star*, Swiss Edition, 2006, no. 65, 7.

Chapter 6

1. David Lionel Salomons, *Breguet (1747–1823)* (London: Salomons, 1921), 8–9.
2. *Le Monde*, 29 June 1967 and 31 May 1969.
3. *Le Droit*, July 4 1870.
4. *Le Droit*, October 7 1881.
5. *Archives commerciales de la France*, 14 July 1886.
6. *Le Figaro*, 25 December 1921.
7. 'Montres Breguet SA', *International Directory of Company Histories* 196 (2018), 297.
8. Ibid.
9. *Indicateur Davoine*, 1950, 357; Christie's, https://www.christies.com/en/lot/lot-6185732 (accessed 2 February 2024).
10. François Bodet, *Breguet, the story of a passion, 1973–1987* (La Croix: Watchprint, 2015).
11. Bodet, 25–7.
12. Bodet, 34.
13. *FOSC*, 10 May 1974.
14. Bodet, 38; *Le Figaro*, 23 February 2023. Munz, 138.
15. Bodet, 43.
16. *FOSC*, 23 October 1980. The three Swiss partners of Chaumet brothers, Roger Dunant, Joseph Goetschmann and Alain Layat, were engaged in numerous financial and real estate companies in Switzerland. They stayed on the board of Montres Breguet SA until its takeover by Investcorp in 1987.
17. Bodet, 40–1.
18. Bodet, 45.
19. George Daniels, *The Art of Breguet* (London: Sotheby Parke Bernet Publications, 1975; second edition by Philip Wilson Publishers, 2021).
20. George Daniels, L'œuvre d'Abraham-Louis Breguet, Catalogue de l'exposition du Musée international d'horlogerie (La Chaux-de-Fonds: MIH, 1976).
21. *L'Impartial*, 28 January 1976.
22. https://quillandpad.com/2015/12/18/book-review-breguet-the-story-of-a-passion-1973-1987/
23. Bodet, 65.
24. Karina Pronitcheva, 'Luxury brands and public museums: from anniversary exhibitions to co-branding', *Global Luxury: Organizational Change and Emerging Markets since the 1970s* (2018): 219–37.
25. *Trade Bulletin*, 1983, no. 965, 5.
26. Bodet, 61.
27. Bodet, 62–3.
28. *Journal de Genève*, 1 May 1987.
29. *Journal de Genève*, 8 June 1987.
30. *Journal de Genève*, 7 and 15 July 1987.

31. *Les Echos*, 21 October 1999.
32. *FOSC*, 7 December 1989.
33. *FOSC*, 25 February 1992 and 10 August 1992.
34. *FOSC*, 30 May 1996.
35. *FOSC*, 3 December 1987.
36. *FOSC*, 16 December 1992.
37. Catherine Cardinal and Pierre Imhof, *Trésors du Musée international d'horlogerie la Chaux-de-Fonds Suisse* (Paris: Le Louvre des Antiquaires, 1988).
38. *Europa Star*, Asia Edition, 1987, no. 220, 15.
39. *Europa Star*, Asia Edition, 1991, no. 239, 8.
40. *Europa Star*, Asia Edition, 1991, no. 241, 50.
41. Bodet, op. cit., 80.
42. *Trade Bulletin*, 1992, no. 1057, 4.
43. Ibid.
44. The 1990s was a decade of consolidation through the verticalization of suppliers of components in the Swiss watch industry. Donzé, *A Business History of the Swatch Group*, chapter 4.
45. *FOSC*, 3 January 1918 and 17 October 1991.
46. *FOSC*, 22 July 1992.
47. *FOSC*, 3 June 1981.
48. Bodet, 88.
49. *FOSC*, 13 January 1997.
50. *Europa Star Europe*, no. 224, 1997, 9.
51. Bodet, 84.
52. Emmanuel Breguet, *Breguet horloger depuis 1775*, Paris, 1997; Time and Watches blog, https://www.timeandwatches.com/2022/03/interview-emmanuel-breguet-vice.html (accessed 5 January 2024).
53. Catherine Cardinal (ed.), *Abraham-Louis Breguet, 1747–1823: l'art de mesurer le temps* (La Chaux-de-Fonds: IHT, 1997).
54. *Europa Star Europe*, no. 224, 1997, 9.
55. Donzé, *History of the Swatch Group*.
56. *FOSC*, 23 November 1999.
57. Data for 1999 according to the *Wall Street Journal*, 15 September 1999.
58. Donzé, *Selling Europe to the World*, 19.
59. Donzé, *A Business History of Swatch Group*, 82–3.
60. Vontobel Equity Research, *Vontobel Luxury Goods Shop*, 2011, 55.
61. Swatch Group, Annual report, 2004, 22.
62. *Europa Star Europe*, no. 254, 2002, 72.
63. Swatch Group, Annual report, 2006, 33.
64. Blog Montres de Luxe, https://www.montres-de-luxe.com/La-fabuleuse-histoire-de-la-montre-Breguet-Marie-Antoinette_a2992.html (accessed 5 February 2024).
65. Swatch Group, Annual Report, 2008, 34.

66. Swatch Group, Annual Report, 2004, page 22 and 2009, page 35.
67. Euromonitor International, Passport database, accessed 13 April 2020.
68. Swatch Group, Annual Report, 2014, page 33 and 2016, page 14.
69. Swatch Group, Annual Report, 40.
70. Swatch Group, Annual Report, 2018, 20.
71. Swatch Group, Annual Report, 2016, 40.
72. Europa Star website, https://www.europastar.com/time-business/1004092985-breguet-appoints-lionel-a-marca-as-its-new-ceo.html (accessed 5 February 2024).
73. Donzé, *The Business of Time*; Alun C. Davies, *The Rise and Decline of England's Watchmaking Industry, 1550–1930* (London and New York: Routledge, 2022).
74. Passion Horlogère, 13 April 2013, https://passion-horlogere.com/eric-loth-fondateur-de-graham-sa/ et Europa Star Watch Files, July 2018, https://www.europastar.com/the-watch-files/the-digital-transformation-of-watchmaking/1004090309-mechanical-smartwatches.html (accessed 15 January 2024).
75. *Europa Star Europe*, no. 230, 1998, 12.
76. *FOSC*, 6 April 1995.
77. Ibid.
78. Donzé, *A Business History of the Swatch Group*, 66–7.
79. *FOSC*, 1 September 1988, *Europa Star Europe*, no. 230, 1998, 14.
80. *FOSC*, various volumes.
81. Herbert Cescinsky, *The Old English Master Clockmakers and Their Clocks, 1670–1820* (New York: Frederick A. Stokes Company, 1938).
82. *Europa Star Europe*, no. 236, 1999, 14.
83. *FOSC*, 1 February 1974.
84. *FOSC*, 1 May 1990 and 31 May 1990.
85. Europa Star Timekeeper, October 2003, https://www.europastar.com/news/2037697-the-jaquet-case-stirs-turmoil-in-the-watch-world.html (accessed 15 January 2024).
86. *Europa Star Europe*, no. 236, 1999, 16.
87. *Europa Star Europe*, no. 236, 1999, 14.
88. *Europa Star Europe*, no. 243, 2000, 90.
89. *FOSC*, 21 August 2000.
90. *Europa Star Europe*, no. 254, 2002, 36.
91. *Europa Star Europe*, no. 285, 2007, 67.
92. *Europa Star Europe*, no. 283, 2007, page 42 and no. 285, 2007, page 68.
93. *FOSC*, 13 September 2001 and 25 April 2002.
94. *Europa Star Europe*, no. 246, 2001, 178.
95. Cescinsky.
96. *FOSC*, 20 February 2002.
97. *Trade Bulletin*, no. 1163, 2007, 20–1.
98. *Europa Star Europe*, no. 302, 2010, 28–9.
99. *FOSC*, 17 October 2019.
100. *FOSC*, 29 July 2010 and 12 April 2012.

101. *Europa Star Europe*, no. 327, 2014, 24.
102. *FOSC*, 6 December 2010.
103. *Europa Star Europe*, no. 312, 2012, 106.
104. *Europa Star Europe*, no. 318, 84.
105. *Europa Star Europe*, no. 236, 2014, 34.
106. The ranking for the year 2017 includes 64 brands over 15 million CHF of gross sales, but neither Arnold & Son nor Graham are mentioned.
107. *Le Temps*, 13 March 2012.
108. Marie-Jeanne Liengme, *Le sens de la mesure: L'émergence d'un discours historique centré sur l'horlogerie neuchâteloise* (Neuchâtel: Cahiers de l'Institut d'histoire, 1994); Laurence Marti, *L'invention de l'horloger* (Lausanne: Antipodes, 2003).
109. *FOSC*, 20 December 1961. The company took the name of Aquastar Instruments SA in 1982 and was liquidated in 2019. Source: Registre du commerce, Geneva, https://app2.ge.ch/ecohrcinternet/ (accessed 7 January 2024).
110. *Europa Star Europe*, no. 137, 1983, 34.
111. *FOSC*, 12 February 1988. This financial company was not officially registered and does not appear in *FOSC* except regarding the purchase of the Jean Richard brand. Its address was Rue du Rhône 100, in a building that hosts numerous small financial companies. Moro's dead body was found in 1993 in a lake in the canton of Fribourg. *Le Nouveau Quotidien*, 30 April 1993.
112. *FOSC*, 20 April 1988.
113. *FOSC*, 15 October 1990 and 17 December 1990.
114. *FOSC*, 22 November 1990 and 23 January 1987; *Europa Star Europe*, vol. 132, 95. Grenier left the board of Nouvelle Lemania in 1985 (*FOSC*, 11 March 1985).
115. *FOSC*, 26 May 1993 and 12 December 1994.
116. *FOSC*, 7 October 1996.
117. *FOSC*, 20 February 1996.
118. *Europa Star Europe*, no. 221, 1997, 143.
119. *Europa Star Europe*, no. 230, 1998, 23.
120. *Europa Star Europe*, no. 230, 1998, 23.
121. *Europa Star Switzerland*, no. 24, 2003, 3.
122. *Europa Star Europe*, no. 317, 2011, 53.
123. *Europa Star Europe*, no. 317, 2011, 53.
124. *Le Temps*, 12 June 2008.
125. *Le Temps*, 17 January 2012.
126. *Europa Star Europe*, no. 317, 2011, 53.
127. *Europa Star Europe*, no. 323, 2014, 12.
128. *Europa Star Europe*, no, 330, 2015, 37.
129. *Europa Star*, Watch Files, 'Resurrecting brands has proved vital for the Swiss watch industry', May 2023.
130. WIPO Global Brands Database, https://branddb.wipo.int/ (accessed 28 February 2024); *FOSC*, 21 December 2012.

131. Pierre-Yves Donzé, 'Un horloger genevois de la première partie du XIXe siècle: François Czapek', *Chronometrophilia* 81 (2017): 96–103; Foulkes, chapters 1 and 2.
132. Antiquorum, https://catalog.antiquorum.swiss/en/lots/lot-100-175?browse_all=1&page=1&q=Czapek (accessed 2 March 2023).
133. *FOSC*, 15 April 2005.
134. *Europa Star Switzerland*, vol. 97, 2015, 18.
135. *Europa Star Global Edition*, vol. 353, 2019, 83.
136. *Europa Star Global Edition*, vol. 353, 2019, 83.
137. WIPO, Global Brands Database.
138. European patent office, Espacenet database, patents no. CH182'127 and CH185'165, https://worldwide.espacenet.com/ (accessed 4 June 2024).
139. There is no mention of any official record of a Lowenthal watch brand in *FOSC*, and this name is not mentioned in Davoine directories. It is, however, mentioned as a brand owned by Bovet on the website Mikrolisk dedicated to trademarks. See www.mikrolisk.de (accessed 12 March 2024).
140. Philip Kuchel, 'Independent-train watches and jump quarter-seconds: An explanation of how they work', *Horological Journal* (October 2015): 442–6; *Antiquarian Horology* 8 (1972): 412–13.
141. WIPO, Global Brand Database; Registre du commerce, canton of Neuchâtel.
142. On Parisian haute couture, see Véronique Pouillard, *Paris to New York: The Transatlantic Fashion Industry in the Twentieth Century* (Cambridge, MA: Harvard University Press, 2021).

Bibliography

Archives

Archives Longines, Saint-Imier.
Musée international d'horlogerie (MIH), La Chaux-de-Fonds, Archives de l'horlogerie.
MIH, Indicateur Davoine. Published sources.

Published sources

Archives commerciales de la France.
Citychamps, Annual Reports.
Le Droit.
Les Echos.
Egana Goldpfeil, Annual Report.
Feuille officielle Suisse du commerce (FOSC).
Le Figaro.
Financial Times.
Gazette de Lausanne.
L'Hebdo.
Helvea, *The Swatch Group*, 2007.
L'Impartial.
JETRO, *Suisu no kinzokusei tokei bando shijo chosa*, Osaka: JETRO, 1982.
Journal de Genève.
Journal du Jura.
Journal suisse d'horlogerie.
Los Angeles Times.
LVMH, Annual Report.
Le Monde.
Montres Passion.
Morgan Stanley Research.
Movado, Annual Report (Form 10-K).
New York Times.
Nikkei Asia.

Le Nouveau Quotidien.

Rapport de la Commission pour l'étude des prix, *Etude critique des conditions de concurrence dans l'industrie horlogère suisse*, March 1959.

Statistiques historiques de la Suisse.

Swatch Group, Annual Report.

Le Temps.

Trinity, Annual Report.

Vontobel Equity Research.

Wall Street Journal.

Internet sources

Cambridge Dictionary, https://dictionary.cambridge.org/
Chanel, https://www.chanel.com/us/about-chanel/the-founder/
Dictionnaire historique de la Suisse, https://hls-dhs-dss.ch/fr/
Dictionnaire du Jura, www.diju.ch
Elsa Schiaparelli, https://www.schiaparelli.com
Espacenet Database, https://worldwide.espacenet.com/
Euromonitor International, Passport database, www.portal.euromonitor.com/
Europa Star, https://www.europastar.com/club.html
Fashion Network, https://fr.fashionnetwork.com/
Institut National de la Propriété Intellectuelle (INPI), https://data.inpi.fr/
Swiss Diplomatic Documents Database (Dodis), https://www.dodis.ch/en
WIPO Global Brands Database, https://branddb.wipo.int/

Books and articles

Allères, Danielle, 'Spécificités et stratégies marketing des différents univers du luxe', *Revue française du marketing* 8 (1991): 115–46.

Hamida, Aman, *L'évolution de la communication publicitaire: le cas de l'entreprie Ebel de 1911 à 2001*, University of Lausanne, unpublished master thesis, 2002.

Blanc, Jean-François, *Suisse-Hong Kong, le défi horloger*, Lausanne: Editions d'En-bas, 1988.

Blancpain, Claude, *La famille Blancpain*, Nonan-sur-Matran Fribourg: C. Blancpain, 1994.

Bodet, François, *Breguet, the story of a passion, 1973–1987*, La Croix: Watchprint, 2015.

Borloz, Jean, *100 ans Office fédéral de la propriété intellectuelle*, Bern: Bundesamt für Geistiges Eigentum, 1988.

Boutillier, Sophie, and Dimitri Uzunidis, 'Entrepreneurs historiques de l'industrie du luxe et innovation permanente', *Innovations* 2 (2013): 91–115.

Brachet Champsaur, Florence, 'Madeleine Vionnet and Galeries Lafayette: The unlikely marriage of a Parisian couture house and a French department store, 1922–40', *Business History* 54, 1 (2012): 48–66.

Breguet, Emmanuel, *Breguet horloger depuis 1775*, Paris: Alain De Gourcuff, 1997.

Briselance, Claude, *Les écoles d'horlogerie de Besançon: une contribution décisive au développement industriel local et régional (1793–1974)*, Université de Lyon II, unpublished PhD dissertation, 2015.

Cardinal, Catherine (ed.), *Abraham-Louis Breguet, 1747–1823: l'art de mesurer le temps*, La Chaux-de-Fonds: IHT, 1997.

Cardinal, Catherine and Pierre Imhof, *Trésors du Musée international d'horlogerie la Chaux-de-Fonds Suisse*, Paris: Le Louvre des Antiquaires, 1988.

Carr, Edward H., *What is History?*, Cambridge: Cambridge University Press, 1961.

Cartier Brickell, Francesca, *Cartier: The Untold Story of the Family Behind the Jewelry Empire*, New York: Ballantine Books, 2019.

Cescinsky, Herbert, *The Old English Master Clockmakers and Their Clocks, 1670–1820*, New York: Frederick A. Stokes Company, 1938.

Chachereau, Nicolas, *Les débuts du système suisse des brevets d'invention (1873–1914)*, Neuchâtel: Alphil, 2022.

Chandler, Alfred, *Scale and Scope Scale and Scope: The dynamics of industrial capitalism*, Cambridge, MA: Harvard University Press, 1990.

Daniels, George, *The Art of Breguet*, London: Sotheby Parke Bernet Publications, 1975 (second edition by Philip Wilson Publishers, 2021).

Daniels, George, *L'œuvre d'Abraham-Louis Breguet, Catalogue de l'exposition du Musée international d'horlogerie*, La Chaux-de-Fonds: MIH, 1976.

Davies, Alun C., *The Rise and Decline of England's Watchmaking Industry, 1550–1930*. London: Routledge, 2022.

Dion, Delphine, 'How to manage heritage brands: The case of sleeping beauties revival', in Pierre-Yves Donzé, Véronique Pouillard and Joanne Roberts (eds), *Oxford Handbook of Luxury Business*, New York: Oxford University Press, 2022, pp. 273–86.

Dion, Delphine, and Gérald Mazzalovo, 'Reviving sleeping beauty brands by rearticulating brand heritage', *Journal of Business Research* 69, no.12 (2016): 5894–900.

Donzé, Pierre-Yves, *History of the Swiss Watch Industry from Jacques David to Nicolas Hayek*, Berne: Peter Lang, third edition, 2011.

Donzé, Pierre-Yves, 'Global competition and technological innovation: A new interpretation of the watch crisis, 1970s–1980s', in David Thomas, Jon Mathieu, Janick Marina Schaufelbuehl and Tobias Straumann (eds), *Crises – Causes, Interpretations and Consequences*, Zurich: Chronos, 2012, pp. 275–89.

Donzé, Pierre-Yves, *A Business History of the Swatch Group: The Rebirth of Swiss Watchmaking and the Globalization of the Luxury Industry*, Basingstoke: Palgrave Macmillan, 2014.

Donzé, Pierre-Yves, *Industrial Development, Technology Transfer, and Global Competition: The Japanese Watch Industry from 1850 to the Present Day*, New York: Routledge, 2017.

Donzé, Pierre-Yves, 'Fashion watches: The emergence of accessory makers as intermediaries in the fashion system', *International Journal of Fashion Studies* 4, no. 1 (2017): 73–4.

Donzé, Pierre-Yves, *L'invention du luxe: histoire de l'horlogerie à Genève de 1815 à nos jours*, Neuchâtel: Alphil, 2017.

Donzé, Pierre-Yves, 'Un horloger genevois de la première partie du XIXe siècle: François Czapek', *Chronometrophilia*, no. 81, 2017, pp. 96–103.

Donzé, Pierre-Yves, 'National labels and the competitiveness of European industries: The example of the "Swiss Made" law since 1950', *European Review of History* 26, no. 5 (2019): 855–70.

Donzé, Pierre-Yves, 'The transformation of global luxury brands: The case of the Swiss watch company Longines, 1880–2010', *Business History* 62, no. 1 (2020): 26–41.

Donzé, Pierre-Yves, 'Industrial leadership and the long-lasting competitiveness of the Swiss watch industry', in Guttmann Martin (ed.), *Historians on Leadership and Strategy: Case Studies from Antiquity to Modernity*, Cham: Springer, 2020, pp. 171–91.

Donzé, Pierre-Yves,'La transformation de l'horlogerie suisse en industrie du luxe', in Blancheton Bertrand (ed.), *Vers le haut de gamme made in France*, Paris: Histoire économique et financière de la France, 2021, pp. 181–98.

Donzé, Pierre-Yves, *The Business of Time: Global History of the Watch Industry*, Manchester: Manchester University Press, 2022.

Donzé Pierre-Yves, *Selling Europe to the World: The Rise of the Luxury Fashion Industry, 1980–2020*, London: Bloomsbury, 2023.

Donzé, Pierre-Yves, *The Making of a Status Symbol: A Business History of Rolex*, Manchester: Manchester University Press, 2025.

Donzé, Pierre-Yves, and Ben Wubs, 'Storytelling and the Making of a Global Luxury Fashion Brand: Christian Dior', *International Journal of Fashion Studies* 6, no. 1 (2019): 83–102.

Donzé, Pierre-Yves, and Ben Wubs, 'LVMH: Storytelling and organizing creativity in luxury and fashion', in Regina Lee Blaszczyk and Véronique Pouillard (eds), *European Fashion*, Manchester: Manchester University Press, 2020, pp. 63–85.

Emch, Arlette-Elsa, *Léon Hatot*, Paris: Assouline, 2005.

Fine Jewels and Watches from the Atelier of Leon Hatot, Geneva: Christie's, 1989.

Foulkes, Nicholas, *Patek Philippe: le biographie autorisée*, London: Preface, 2016.

Gagnebin-Diacon, Christine, *La fabrique et le village: la Tavannes Watch Co. (1890–1918)*, Porrentruy: CEH, 1996.

Garelick, Rhonda. 'Lagerfeld, fashion, and cultural heritage', *English Language Notes* 60, no. 2 (2022): 156–74.

Grau, François-Marie, *La haute couture*, Paris: PUF, 2000.

Grumbach, Didier, *History of International Fashion*, Northampton: Interlink Books, 2014.

Henry Bédat, Jacqueline, *Une région, une passion: l'horlogerie. Une entreprise: Longines*, Saint-Imier: Compagnie des Montres Longines Francillon, 1992.

Higgins, David M., *Brands, Geographical Origin, and the Global Economy: A History from the Nineteenth Century to the Present*, Cambridge: Cambridge University Press, 2018.

Hobsbawm, Eric, and Terence Ranger (eds), *The Invention of Tradition*, Cambridge: Cambridge University Press, 1983.

Hogan, Michael J., ed., *Hiroshima in History and Memory*, Cambridge: Cambridge University Press, 1996.

'Investcorp SA', *International Directory of Company Histories*, Gale, 2004, vol. 57, pp. 179–82.

Jeannerat, Hugues, and Olivier Crevoisier, 'Non-technological innovation and multi-local territorial knowledge dynamics in the Swiss watch industry', *International Journal of Innovation and Regional Development* 3, no. 1 (2011): 26–44.

Jones, Geoffrey, *Multinationals and Global Capitalism: From the Nineteenth to the Twenty-First Century*, New York: Oxford University Press, 2005.

Jones, Geoffrey, *Beauty Imagined: A History of the Global Beauty Industry*, New York: Oxford University Press, 2010.

Jones, Geoffrey, *Deeply Responsible Business: A Global History of Values-Driven Leadership*, Cambridge, MA: Harvard University Press, 2023.

Jones, Geoffrey, and Emily Grandjean, *Coco Chanel: From Fashion Icon to Nazi Agent*, Cambridge, MA: Harvard Business School, case no. 9-318-139, 2023.

Kapferer, Jean-Noël, 'The post-global brand', *Journal of Brand Management* 12, no. 5 (2005): 319–24.

Kapferer, Jean-Noël, and Vincent Bastien, *The Luxury Strategy: Break the Rules of Marketing to Build Luxury Brands*, London: Kogan Page, 2012.

Král, Petr. 'Could there be a luxury brand originating from the Czech Republic? The case of the Czech watchmaker Prim', *Central European Business Review* 2, no. 3 (2013): 15–21.

Kuchel, Philip, 'Independent-train watches and jump quarter-seconds: An explanation of how they work', *Horological Journal* (October 2015): 442–6.

Levitt, Theodore, 'The globalization of markets', *Harvard Business Review* 61 (1983): 3.

Liengme, Marie-Jeanne, *Le sens de la mesure: L'émergence d'un discours historique centré sur l'horlogerie neuchâteloise*, Neuchâtel: Cahiers de l'Institut d'histoire, 1994.

Linder, Patrick, *Longines, un sablier et des ailes: histoire, enjeux, construction d'une marque: 120 ans de la protection d'un logotype (1889–2009)*, Saint-Imier: Longines, 2009.

Lopes, Teresa da Silva, *Global Brands: The Evolution of Multinationals in Alcoholic Beverages*, New York: Cambridge University Press, 2007.

Lopes, Teresa da Silva, Bruna Dourado, and Elizabeth Santos de Souza, 'Unbundling the brand: Differentiation and the law in the Brazilian South American tea industry', *Business History* (2022): 1–24.

Marrou, Henri-Irénée, *De la connaissance historique*, Paris: Seuil, 1954.

Marti, Laurence, *L'invention de l'horloger*, Lausanne: Antipodes, 2003.

Marti, Laurence, *Une région au rythme du temps: Histoire socio-économique du Vallon de Saint-Imier, 1700–2007*, Saint-Imier: Edition des Longines, 2007.

Bibliography

Martin-Achard, Edmond, 'La nationalité Suisse de la montre', *La semaine judiciaire* 81, no. 10 (1959): 145–67.

Moore, Christopher M., and Grete Birtwistle, 'The nature of parenting advantage in luxury fashion retailing: The case of Gucci group NV', *International Journal of Retail & Distribution Management* 33, no. 4 (2005): 256–70.

Moore, Karl, and Susan Reid, 'The birth of brand: 4000 years of branding', *Business History* 50, no. 4 (2008): 419–32.

Mora, Juliana Luna, and Jess Berry, 'Creative direction succession in luxury fashion: The illusion of immortality at Chanel and Alexander McQueen', *Luxury* (2023): 1–24.

Munz, Hervé, *La transmission en jeu: apprendre, pratiquer, patrimonialiser: l'horlogerie en Suisse*, Neuchâtel: Alphil, 2016.

Munz, Hervé, 'Crafting time, making luxury: The heritage system and artisan revival in the Swiss watch industry, 1975–2015', in Pierre-Yves Donzé and Rika Fujioka (eds), *Global Luxury: Organizational Change and Emerging Markets since the 1970s*, Singapore: Palgrave Macmillan, 2018: 197–218.

Pasche, Jean-Daniel, *La protection des armoiries fédérales et de l'indication 'suisse'*, Neuchâtel: Editions Ides et Calendes, 1988.

Patek Philippe 175, Geneva: Christie's, 2014.

Pouillard, Véronique, *Paris to New York: The Transatlantic Fashion Industry in the Twentieth Century*, Cambridge, MA: Harvard University Press, 2021.

Prongué, Bernard (ed.), *L'écartèlement: espace jurassien et identité plurielle*, Saint-Imier: Canevas, 1991.

Pronitcheva, Karina, 'Luxury brands and public museums: From anniversary exhibitions to co-branding', in Pierre-Yves Donzé and Rika Fujioka (eds), *Global Luxury: Organizational Change and Emerging Markets since the 1970s*, Singapore: Palgrave Macmillan, 2018: 219–37.

Richon, Marco, *Omega Saga*, Biel: Fondation Brandt, 1998.

Sáiz, Patricio, and Rafael Castro, 'Trademarks in branding: Legal issues and commercial practices', *Business History* 60, no. 8 (2018): 1105–26.

Sáiz, Patricio, and Rafael Castro, eds, *The Brand and Its History: Trademarks, Branding and National Identity*, London: Routledge, 2022.

Salomons, David Lionel, *Breguet (1747–1823)*, London: Salomons, 1921.

Scheufele, Karl-Friedrich, 'Postface', in Denise Kenyon-Rouvinez and John L. Ward (eds), *Family Business: Key Issues*, Basingstoke: Palgrave Macmillan, 2005, p. 77.

Schmid, Hans-Heinrich, *Lexikon der Deutschen Uhrenindustrie 1850–1980*. Nuremberg: German Society for Chronometrie, vol. 2, 2017.

Schwarzkopf, Stefan, 'Turning trademarks into brands: How advertising agencies practiced and conceptualized branding, 1890–1930', in Stefan Schwarzkopf (ed.), *Trademarks, Brands, and Competitiveness*, New York: Routledge, 2010, pp. 187–215.

Seyffer, David, *Die Unternehmensgeschichte von IWC Schaffhausen: Ein Schweizer Uhrenhersteller zwischen Innovation und Tradition*, Oberhausen: Athena Verlag, 2014.

Speckhart, Gustav, *Peter Henlein der Erfinder der Taschenuhr: fachgeschichtliche Abhandlung*, Nuremberg: Verl. J.L., 1890.

Steele, Valerie, *Paris Fashion: A cultural history*, Oxford: Oxford University Press, 1988.

Trubert-Tollu, Chantal, Françoise Tétart-Vittu, Jean-Marie Martin-Hattemberg and Fabrice Olivieri, *The House of Worth, 1858–1954: The Birth of Haute Couture*, London: Thames & Hudson, 2017.

Trueb, Lucien F., *The world of watches; history, technology, industry*, New York: Ebner Publishing, 2005.

Tungate, Mark. *Luxury World: The Past, Present and Future of Luxury Brands*, London: Kogan Page, 2009.

Urde, Mats, Stephen A. Greyser and John M. T. Balmer. 'Corporate brands with a heritage,' *Journal of Brand Management* 15 (2007): 4–19.

Viredaz, Michel, 'Léon Hatot et les horloges électriques ATO', *Chronométrophilia*, no. 56 (2004): 67–77.

Wimmer-Olbort, Iris, *1904–2004: Karl Scheufele: une entreprise familiale au fil du temps*, Paris: Le Petit-Fils de L.U. Chopard & Cie S.A., 2004.

Zanon, Johanna, 'Reawakening the "sleeping beauties" of haute couture: The case of Guy and Arnaud de Lummen', Regina Lee Blaszczyk and Véronique Pouillard (eds), *European Fashion: The Creation of a Global Industry*, Manchester: Manchester University Press, 2020, pp. 86–116.

Index

A. Lange & Söhne 22, 66–70, 129, 133–4
Antiquorum 31, 52, 80, 115, 124–5
Arnault, Bernard 6–7, 10, 13, 15
Arnold & Son 114–8, n154
Artemis 11
Audemars Piguet 1, 23–6, 31, 54–6, 68, 72, 80, 104, 113, 116, 129

Bader, Thépohile 7
Balmain, Pierre 7
Bannwart, Jean-René 93
Bannwart, René 40, 93
Baselworld Watch Fair 62, 91, 112, 125
Bennahmias François-Henry 1, 26
Bertin, Rose 5
Big Bang 91
Biver, Jean-Claude 20–2, 54–7, 59–60, 72, 87, 90–2, 100, 109, 119, n144
Blancpain 20, 46, 50, 52–60, 69, 72, 87, 90, 109, 115, 119, 133–5, n 144
Blum, Pierre-Alain 96–7
Blümlein, Günter 68
Bodet, François 104–5, 107, 109
Bovet 52, 127–8, n 155
Breguet 9, 22, 24–5, 59–60, 101–13, 115, 119, 124, 131, 133–5, n 151
Breguet, Abraham-Louis 102–3, 105–6
Breitling 2, 24, 73–4
Bourdieu, Pierre 13
Boussac Group 6, 13
Bulgari 2, 16, 23–5, 50, 59, 63, 65, 86

Calabrese, Vincent 52, 59, 93
Calatrava 19, 26, 78–79, 100, 134
Cartier 2, 12, 16, 18–19, 22–5, 31, 54, 60, 65, 67, 70, 73–4, 81, 86, 96
Cerruti 1881 8
Chanel 13, 15, 23, 25, 73
Chéruit 7
Chaumet 9, 97, 10, 104–5, 107, 134, n 151

China Haidian, *see* Citychamp Watch & Jewelry Group
Chopard 2, 19, 24, 59, 63, 65, 75, 81–6, 100, 104, 133–4, n 148
Chopard, Louis-Ulysse 81
Christian Dior, *see* Dior
Christie's 60, 62, 79
Corum 93–6, 100, 114, 123, 125
Crocco, Carlo 87, 89–91
Chronode 72, 125, 128, 134
Chronotechna 51
Citychamp Watch & Jewelry Group, 95–6
Citizen Watch 29, 116
Claret, Christophe 115–16
Coach, 97
Compagnie Financière Richemont, *see* Richemont
Courrèges 5, 10–11
Curtit, André 107–8
Cyma 74
Czapek 18, 1247, 131, 133–5

Daniels, George 105
Dior 6–7, 13, 18, 20
Dom Perignon 15
Dress Your Body (DYB) 62–3
Dubuis, Roger 22, 52
Dufour, Philippe 52

Ebel 9, 93, 96–100, 114, 125, 134
Ebohr 96
Egana Goldpfeil 67
Ellicott 116
Elsa Schiaparelli 11
Emch, Arlette-Elsa 62–3, 109
Eterna 96
Excelsior Park 50

Favre & Andrié 36
Favre Brandt 36

Favre, Michel 54
Favre-Leuba 36–7
Fiechter, Jean-Jacques 55
Finazzi, Pierre-André 114–16
Follonier, Sébastien 125
Ford, Tom 5
Frédéric Piguet 54–6, 59

Galeries Lafayette 7
Galliano, John 6–7, 13
Genta, Gérald 50, 93, 104
Gianfranco Ferré 9, 13
Gieves & Hawkes 8
Girard Perregaux 31, 115, 120–1, 123, 125, 131, 134
Glasshütte Original 46
Glashütter Uhrentrieb 66, 68
Graham 114–16, 118, 132–5, n 154
Grand Prix d'Horlogerie de Genève 91, 113, 125
Greubel & Forsey 125
Gucci 5, 9, 17, 24, 95, 97
Guhl, Harry 2, 124–9

Happy Diamonds 82–4, 100, 134
Harry Winston 22, 64–5
Hayek, Marc A. 56, 59, 87, 112–13
Hayek, Nayla 59, 63
Hayek, Nick 62–3, 109
Hayek, Nicolas G. 45, 52, 56, 60, 62, 109, 112–14
Hermès 1, 23–5, 107, 127
Hublot 2, 23–4, 26, 75, 87–92, 100, 133–4
Hugo Boss 97

International Watchmaking Museum 105, 107–9
Investcorp 5, 9, 97, 100, 107–9, 134
Itokin 11
IWC 2, 22, 24, 67, 74

Jaeger-LeCoultre 2, 22, 24, 26, 55, 67, 104, 129
Jaquet Baume 115
Jaquet Droz 22, 60, 119
JeanRichard 101, 119–23, 131, 133, 135
Journe, François-Paul 52, 116
Junghans 51, 66–7
Juvet 52

Känel, Walter von 45
Kanoui, Joseph 73
Kent & Curwen 8
Kering 9, 11, 17, 31, 122–3
Kern, Georges 74
Kokosalaki, Sophia 8

Lacoste 10
Lagerfeld, Karl 13
La Joux Perret 115–16, 134
Lange, Ferdinand Adolph 22, 66–70, 129, 133–4
Léon Hatot 22, 50, 60–5, 72, 133–5, n 144
Les Monts 114–16
Longines 2, 24–5, 38, 40–3, 45–7, 77
L'Oréal 11, 40
Loth, Eric 114–16
Louis Vuitton 16, 18, 23, 25, 50, 56
Lowenthal 124, 126, 128, n 155
Lummen, Guy and Arnaud de 7–10
Luvanis 10
LVMH 8–9, 17–18, 23–5, 29, 50, 91, 97, 107, 123, n 148

Macaluso, Luigi 120–1
Mannesmann 67
Maus Frères 10
Mayhoola for Investments SPC 9
McKinley Tariff Act 39
Merchandise Marks Act 39
Mojon, Jean-François 125, 128
Montres Davidoff 114
Movado Group 97
Moynat 10, 15
Müller, Franck 24, 52, 87

Nivada 50
Nouvelle Lemania 108–9, 111, 119, n 154

Officine Panerai 2, 24
Omega 2, 20–4, 28, 38, 40, 43, 54, 56, 58, 60, 64, 70, 77, 90, 93, 108–9

Paquin 12
Paris Group 9
Parmigiani, Michel 52, 84, 87, 114
Patek Philippe 2, 12, 18–19, 24–6, 31, 34, 49, 74, 76–80, 93, 100, 102, 109, 113, 124, 129, 133–4

Perrin, Alain-Dominique 73
Pfeifer, Heinz W. 68–9
Piaget 19, 22, 24, 63, 65, 67, 81–2, 86, 114
Piguet, Jacques 54
Poljot 51
Pouzait 124, 128–31
Pronto Watch 74

Rado 24–5, 46
Raketa 51
Raymond Weil 20, 24, 52
Rayville 53–5
Renaud & Papi 68–9, 72
Renown 8
Richard Mille 1, 5, 24–6, 68, 87
Richemont 17, 19, 22–4, 26, 31, 50, 56, 67–68, 72–73, 123, 134, n 148
Robergé Watches 20, 52
Roberto Cavalli 9
Rossini 96
Rotary 96
Roth, Daniel 50, 104–05
Roquemaurel, Xavier de 124–5
Rolex 1, 20–21, 23–25, 38, 40, 43, 45, 49, 58, 74, 77, 80, 89, 102–4

Samsung 29–30, 42–3
Scheufele, Caroline 82, 84
Scheufele, Karl 81–2
Scheufele, Karl-Friedrich 82, 84
Schneider, Ernest 74
Seiko 21, 42, 52
Shandong Ruyi 8
Shinsegae International 8, 10
Sicura 74
Société Suisse de Microélectronique et d'Horlogerie (SMH), *see* Swatch Group

Société Suisse pour l'industrie horlogère (SSIH) 43, 54, 108
Sofisti, Michele 123
Solvil & Titus 74
Stein, Alfred G. 76
Stelux Holdings International 74
Stern, family 19, 49, 75–6, 78–9
Swatch 1, 18, 21, 25, 27, 45, 59
Swatch Group 9, 20–2, 24–5, 28, 30–1, 43, 45–6, 50, 52, 56, 59–60, 62–5, 69–72, 84, 87, 109, 111–14, 123, 134, n 144
Swiss Made 43–4, 70, 74, 96

TAG Heuer 2, 12, 23–5, 29, 97
Tavannes Watch 78
The British Masters of Timekeeping 115
Thomke, Ernst 114
Tiffany 9, 12, 16, 19, 22, 63, 65, 76, 81, 86, 97
Tissot 2, 24, 29, 46, 54, 71
Tod's 11
Tommy Hilfiger 97
Trinity Group 8, 73

Vacheron Constantin (Vacheron & Constantin) 2, 18, 22, 24, 34, 67, 77, 104
Valentino 9
Van Cleef & Arpels 22, 65, 68, 86
Vionnet 7–9
Vision Investment 9

Worth 12
Wunderman, Severin 95, 100

Zenith 23, 38, 43